Chance Meetings

STORIES ABOUT CROSS-CULTURAL KARMIC COLLISIONS AND COMPASSION

Madhu Bazaz Wangu

Website: www.Mindful-Writers.com
Twitter: @Madhu_Wangu

This book is a work of fiction. Names, characters, places, and incidents are products of the author's imagination or are used fictitiously. Any resemblance to actual events or locations or persons, living or dead, is entirely coincidental.

Cover Design: Natasha Brown

ISBN: 978-1-64649-348-7
eISBN: 978-1-64649-349-4
LCCN: 2014917482

A LIST OF STORIES

FOREWORD 5
CYCLE OF LIFE 13
CADMIUM AND CRIMSON 21
SECRET HEALER 41
AN AMERICAN DIALOGUE 81
GAURI'S FREEDOM 101
THE BLACKENED MIRROR 149
THE THUG 169
A PRECIOUS GIFT 179
A CHANCE MEETING 193
YELLOW JACKET 211
DARKNESS BEHIND EYES 225
PORTABLE SHRINE 247
CHAPTER ONE An Immigrant Wife 267

FOREWORD

"You are what your deep, driving desire is. As your desire is, so is your will. As your will is, so is your deed, as your deed is, so is your destiny."

(Bhrihadaranyaka Upanishad IV.4.5)

Part story, part memoir, *Chance Meetings: Stories About Cross-Cultural Karmic Collisions and Compassion* is inspired by my life as an artist, a professor of Indian art history, a writer, and a dilettante commentator of Asian scriptures. My interest in writing stories was stirred when I had a driving desire to express what I had learned from the various lives I have lived. The diverse tracks that I had followed until my early-fifties coalesced and stimulated these stories and my debut novel, *An Immigrant Wife*.

I graduated from Art College with an under-graduate degree in Studio Arts and a Masters in Art History. For a decade I worked as a freelance artist. I painted landscapes and life-size portraits and made woodcut prints. During this period, I had five one-person exhibitions in India and in the United States, where I had emigrated after marriage.

As a painter, I feel that the process of painting and the painting itself are linked with an invisible source that stimulates creative flow and aesthetic pleasure. The source, only a hairbreadth away from me, infuses artworks with unique vitality that gives them a life of their own.

Three stories in *Chance Meetings* were sparked from my painting period. Aspiring artists come across colossal blocks on the creative path. They face resentment and rejection from their family circle. Friends and relatives look upon them with pitying condescension. They are chastised for wasting time in a fruitless pursuit. The protagonist of "Gauri's Freedom" struggles to pacify and overcome rebuff from her family but in vain. In "The Blackened Mirror," the fame and fortune a painter dreams about becomes a reality only to reveal its destructive side. Jealousy and competitiveness is the dominant emotion in "Cadmium and Crimson." But this story was also prompted by another experience. More about that later.

After living in the United States for years, I joined the doctoral program in the Phenomenology of Religion. I had to stop painting to study for my preliminary examination. The month I passed my exams my youngest brother was killed in an automobile accident in India. A few months after my mother passed away, and a year later my father died. My world turned upside down. A flood of swirling emotions overcame me. Nothing seemed stable. No clear outlines. No vivid color. Food tasted like ash. No music could reach my ears nor smells my nose. I must have been breathing because I was not dead.

The thought of my own demise and those closest to me was crippling. The sharp-toothed snare of death was sinister. Annihilation seemed close at hand. I could lose any one at any time. Without notice, life can take away the people I love. My husband's business flights to different states froze my heart. Minutes of delay of our daughters' school bus numbed my legs.

I kept myself occupied with research, reading, and writing. Time passed and some semblance of normality returned. For my Ph.D. comprehensive exam I chose the topic of death in world cultures: Indian, Chinese, Early American and Aztec. I studied the death symbols, myths and rituals of major world religions. I researched how different cultures dispose of their dead. The new knowledge answered some of my questions. Death is inevitable. After death rituals are meant more for living than the dead. Why some die early no one knows.

It was tragic and uncanny when years later there was a suicide, a murder, and another car accident in our family. Again, it took me some time to absorb the emotions and thoughts that the senseless untimely deaths ignited. But eventually, the negative feelings were pushed down into the darkness of unconscious. After earning a doctoral degree, I began to teach. Eventually, my doctoral dissertation was published as *A Goddess is Born.*

Years later, from the depths of the inner underworld, memories resurfaced and sparked the stories "A Precious Gift," "Yellow Jacket" and parts of "Secret Healer." A normal death seemed desirable. But what was a normal death? Everyone died of something. Which brings me back to "Cadmium and Crimson." This story is also about a serene death. Yet, how many people choose their own coffin and die in peace?

During my research on death, I studied the Hindu goddess Kali. She is one of the seven major North Indian goddesses. Kali's macabre paraphernalia, lolling tongue, disheveled hair, sword in her hand and garland of human skulls around her neck, reflects violence and destruction. But a careful study of symbolic images of the goddess revealed her to be the feminine principle—Dark Earth, bound to the ever-revolving wheel of life-through-death. Her symbols and myths whetted my curiosity and led me to study other Hindu and Buddhist goddesses, popular and local.

My courses on Buddhist and Hindu Art were well received by undergraduate as well as graduate students. Teaching the introductory courses for more than a decade ingrained in me the teachings of Dhammapada, Upanishads, Bhagavad Gita, and Devi Mahatmya (the scripture of the Great Goddess). The teachings not only grounded me in the field of the Phenomenology of Religion but also clarified my mind refining my thoughts about aesthetic and spiritual experiences that cannot be described only experienced such as birthing a child or making love.

In art and literature such experiences are expressed through symbol, simile and metaphors. While teaching history of religious art to college students I found art and spirituality strongly connected. Creative and spiritual experiences were similar, and the infinite joy of these experiences was the same in all world religions.

Answering students' questions about similarities in religious and aesthetic experiences, despite cultural differences, smoothed wrinkles in my mind. The thought that the source of creativity and vitality was only a hairbreadth away was somehow reiterated to me. I learned that to experience the invisible source was a matter of apt attention. What sort of attention? Attention upon what? In the meantime, Facts on File published two of my books for young adults, *Hinduism* (1991) and *Buddhism* (1993).

Every semester I taught one or two courses on religious symbolism in Indian painting and sculpture. In one class while discussing a particular meditating image of the Buddha, (Gupta Period, 5th century, Sarnath) I wondered why the great teacher meditated every single day. I studied Vipassana meditation that the Buddha practiced. Vipassana is an incredibly simple method of meditation, and I too began to practice it daily. Soon I discovered that the practice was simple but not easy. I could not sit still in silence and solitude for more than five minutes.

In 1997 I had an opportunity to teach aboard a ship with the Semester at Sea program at the University of Pittsburgh. For one hundred days I taught Indian, Chinese, and Japanese art and architecture as I voyaged around the world with seven hundred students, twenty-seven faculty members and eighty crewmen.

On the ship I kept a journal and meditated ten to fifteen minutes every day. By then my sitting had somewhat stabilized. As I jotted down my experiences as a teacher-traveler, I did not realize that I was sowing the seed of a novel, *An Immigrant Wife*, and something significant that was going to put me on the path to wisdom and goodness, a way of writing mindfully that I called Mindful Writing Method.

Following the year of the voyage, I felt changed within. But not much had changed without. However, the combination of meditation and journaling worked like magic not only in practice but also in productivity. I published another goddess book, *Images of Indian Goddesses* (2003).

I had given up painting to study history of religious art, but found my inner self wanting something else, "Something More." I decided not to teach in academia. I was in my early fifties. I did not want to retire. I felt re-fired. If not teaching, then what? What would my professional life add up to? *Nothing and Everything! It depends on how you live the rest of your life!* I heard a voice say.

In 2005 I started a website, Spirituality-Sparks, (now renamed www.Mindful-Writers.com) and began to post a weekly commentary titled "As I Understand It." There I discussed Eastern scriptures including Tao Te-Ching, Dhammapada, Bhagavad Gita, and Devi Gita. This drill ingrained in me the significance of an inner life lived thoughtfully.

Raw material from my memories and experiences surfaced that I myself didn't know existed. In meditation I delved deep into the underworld of my mind, and after a period of dealing with the darkness within, I resurfaced with gold nuggets. The dead past wanted to become the living present in the stories I would tell. The memories were transformed into vivid and pulsating tales—imagined, mulled and drafted story lines. From my experiences in India, Japan, and South America were ignited "Secret Healer," "Chance Meeting," and " Portable Shrine."

My daily practice of Vipassana meditation has increased to ninety minutes. As I sit still in silence and solitude, my focus is on my breath. Inhaling and exhaling with awareness has strengthened my attention muscle. The practice of breathing consciously is simultaneously subtle and profound. Ordinarily an involuntary process, breathing is what separates life from death.

The routine of meditation and journaling clears the mind, opens the heart, and energizes me for the rest of the day. Six years ago I began to share the benefits of Mindful Writing Method with professional as well as novice writers. Thus began the idea for a *Mindful Writers Group*, established in 2010. The following year I made my first CD, *Meditations for Mindful Writers*. A *Guidebook for Mindful Writing and Living* is in the works.

Early in my practice I discovered that creative ideas, intuitions, and insights do not come from outside but from what goes on within. The source and ground of all creativity lies deep in me as in all individuals. But my agitated mind and stressed heart had prevented me from this realization. My practice amazes me often when solutions to my problems surge from within.

Daily writing helps me to live a purposeful and peaceful life. Writing is my path and destination. I am dedicated to write books that would not only entertain but also educate and maybe even transform my readers. *Chance Meetings: Stories About Cross-Cultural Karmic Collisions and Compassion* is the first of such endeavors.

Many heartfelt thanks are due to many individuals who helped me bring this book to see the light of the day. Thanks to Jenny Quinlan, my editor, for her insights and helpful suggestions. To Linda Schmitmeyer, for her meticulous copyediting. To Tim Colbert and Cynthia Closkey of Shift Collaborative for the fabulous promotional work they did to bring readers' attention to *Chance Meetings*.

Without Kathleen Shoop's prodding and coaxing, I would not have been persuaded to publish fiction at all! Thank you, Kathie, for your endless support.

To my wonderful friends and first readers: Meredith Mileti, Koyna Sood, Ramona Defelice Long, Candace Banks and Mary Anne Joyal for reading the early drafts of the book and for giving much-needed feedback.

My deeply felt thanks to my daughters, Srimal W. Choi and Zoon Wangu, for your constant encouragement and for making me feel proud to be your mother.

My wholehearted appreciation to my husband, Manoj. You always have and continue to make my dreams come true. Without your support, inspiration, and ideas, my writing would not be what it has become. Thank you!

In closing, to my readers. Thank you for choosing to read this book! Your thoughts and voice matter. As reviews are the new word-of-mouth, if you like the book, please feel free to post a review on www.Amazon.com or www.Barnesandnoble.com

CYCLE OF LIFE

I whimpered and rolled uneasily in my crib. "What an extraordinary wonder of life!" my mother said to no one in particular as she gently touched my cheek, rubbed my earlobe, and patted me back to sleep.

I crawled. I wobbled. I stood up and fell down. Stood up again. I smiled.

I walked. I ran. I danced, and I stood firm on my feet. I read voraciously, consumed books ravenously. I was precocious.

On my fourteenth birthday, I asked my parents what the purpose of life was. They narrowed their eyes. "Purpose of your life!" they said in unison. Their glances met. I repeated, "Yes! Purpose of my life." They asked me to clarify my question. I demanded their answers to simple questions like: Why are we born? Having lived, why do we die? Why do I have to listen to parents and not question my teachers? For a minute, there was silence in the room.

Then, with her eyes wide and hand over her open mouth, my mother muttered something like, "What exceptional inquiries!"

My father said, "Such questions have no answers. Those who seek answers to such questions find their own way. You will understand when you grow up." They both looked amused to hear the questions I had asked earnestly. From that day forward, they kept a closer watch on me.

The eternal river continued to flow under the bridges in our valley. I was in the final year of high school. Scholastic work and seductive events competed with one another. I was appalled by the girls' tittle-tattle about trivialities. I was disgusted by the boys' devil-may-care deeds. I heard their cattiness and malicious talk. In time, these events turned to cobwebs in my mind.

Girls were groomed for home life. Boys were mostly free to do what they wanted. I asked my parents what the point of my growing up was if I could not venture out on my own. Why do boys have leeway while girls have none? Wherever I went, wherever I looked, Brahmins sat in front, Shudras in the back. Would I ever be allowed to choose where I sat? Would I ever be allowed to say where I stood? Again, I heard that piercing silence. Finally, some answers were muttered. Most made no sense—except one. Education is powerful. Education is a weapon. Education has answers.

I went to college to find answers. I thought, like me, other students were also there to seek answers. On the campus, young women and men surrounded me, yet I remained aloof. I felt invisible to them. I liked my own company. I understood the information I received from the books and professors. In silence, I mulled over what I read. I understood why and how birth, life, and death were connected. How all who were born must eventually die. Why bodies must be disposed of one way or the other. Cremation. Burial. Feeding body parts to vultures. Burning bodies. Decaying flesh. Mounds of ash. Bleached bones. New birth.

Too many contradictory and confusing thoughts crammed my head. I poured them out like ink from an overturned inkpot onto my journal. I scribbled all of them down until I had nothing left to write. As soon as a new thought popped in, I put it on paper.

All the nurturing mothers give, the love fathers bestow, the labor of birth, rearing, cherishing, all ends up in nothing. Industriousness through life comes to nothing. Loved ones die. The living grieves. Forgetfulness sets in. Life goes on—the unstoppable flow of the river.

Day in and day out, night after night, in the quiet of my room, I wrote about sorrow and suffering. But I also wrote about delights and pleasure. Were the latter an antidote to the former? Or were they interlacing threads woven into the fabric of my life? Undo the one from the other, and the whole tapestry would fray. Great sages and philosophers had much to say about my questions that were unanswerable, but I understood.

One night, I wrote until the wee hours. I had come to one conclusion: From this very moment, all women should refuse to give birth to new life. No more babies! Save the yet-to-come-generations from all the misery they are bound to confront! Being born is suffering. I wrote commentaries based on the teachings of the wise men and women of the world. Exhausted, I was overcome by sleep.

I smell the ocean. I am walking on white sand. The unfamiliar beach borders the aquamarine ocean. I am carrying fishing net. But I have never fished. I do not intend to fish. I am in search of something. I walk for days. I can't recall what it is that I am looking for.

In the distance, against the dusky sky, I see a silhouette of a village. The beach begins to ascend. Not a soul in sight. When I draw closer, I notice the village appears to be deserted. Higher and higher, I continue on my path, and the village sinks lower and lower. I am at the peak now. Outside one hut, I see a fishing net that holds seashells and conch shells. I want to walk to the net and select the most beautiful ones to take home.

I see the net slipping away with the frothing and foaming of the evening tide. I feel white sand move under my feet. Dusk is ushering in the night. The beach behind me is under water. How will I get back home? Where will I spend the night?

Just one night of rest. In the darkness, someone offers a hand. I feel the warmth of the hand as I am assisted downward. We descend toward a group of huts in a hollow in the ground. We enter a shack. My hand is released. I am fearful. I am afraid of being alone. I have never felt like this before. I am alone in a shack with one lamp. I hear sand falling on the roof. I see the level of the sand rising outside the window. I hear a voice, "Hold the paper umbrella over your seafood soup!" Suddenly, I realize I can't rest. If I don't shovel the whole night, I will be buried alive. I must keep shoveling the sand. If I lay down my shovel, I die.

Individuals die. Dynasties die. Can't find a firm footing anywhere. Am I sinking in quicksand? I imagine my fear being replaced with sand. Sand entering into my nine openings: pelvic, pubic, ear holes, mouth, nostrils, eyes.

I walk out of the hut. The sand blows into my eyes and ears. I want to go back to where I came from. I look up. There is no way out. There is no way to climb back up.

My heart was beating fast when I woke up. I wiped the sweat off my brow. The smell and the sound of the ocean still lingered in the air. My skin smelled of salt. I wrapped a shawl around my shoulders and went for a walk. Breathing in and breathing out, I took each step attentively, deliberately. I forced a smile. I imagined a flower growing with each step where my soles touched the ground. I felt a current pass through me. I felt connected to the earth. The fear seemed to drain through my feet. Absorbed into the earth. I kept walking until my body felt energized, my mind calm, and my heart at peace. On the horizon, the warm glow of the sun winked at me.

In time, I got over the fear I had felt. On one of my morning walks, I saw a man walking in the same direction as I. Our paces matched. He turned his head, nodded, and smiled. As I returned his smile, I noticed his eyes, as clear as water from a mountain stream. He stopped. I stopped. Motionless, we faced each other.

"What a beautiful morning!" he said, his voice like the gentle fall of a fresh stream. "Why have I not seen you before? Do you walk every morning?" he asked. I did not utter a word. I wanted to hear the liquid flow of his voice. I wanted to be with him forever.

Was he the purpose of my life? Did this man have all the answers I was searching for? How could that be? Did I misunderstand? He was saying, asking, telling things to me. I did not hear them. I was attracted to his physique. Charmed by his resplendent face. Mesmerized by his gentle manners. The silence brought me back to my senses. I saw him gazing at me from head to toe.

I wanted to fully grasp the situation, comprehend what was happening, spend a few days understanding my feelings. Before I could do any of that, he asked me if I would consider marrying him. I felt dizzy. My heart beat faster. I realized I was intoxicated with love.

Yes, I would marry him! I would love him for the rest of my life. I could sacrifice my life for him. The passion in his voice rang in my ears. He embraced me. His touch delighted me. He kissed my quivering lips. He kissed me on my neck. And kept kissing me. I forgot who I was. Where I was. What I was doing. Was his love the salve to the suffering of my life?

Soon, I became his bride. In less than a year, I was the mother of the most beautiful baby in the whole universe. When my baby cried, I said to myself, what an extraordinary wonder of life! And gently rubbed her back to sleep, singing the lullaby my mother sang to me.

CADMIUM AND CRIMSON

Valakya vividly remembered a dream that he had the night of his twenty-fifth birthday.

The ebony casket he had carved is on display. From afar, Valakya watches as Mahadevi, the Great Goddess, appraises, admires, scrutinizes. Valakya moves a few steps closer. Cupped in her hands, she holds a blue sphere the size of a peach. He notices a white crane painted on its surface. She extends her arms toward the sky. It starts to rain. First a pitter-patter, then it pours. The crane slowly spreads its wings and soars upward. The rainwater makes the blue of the sphere run. Underneath, the blue shimmering glass ball reflects rainbow colors. In the distance, a gong thunders.

Valakya looks down and sees his feet turn blue. The earth splits, he on the one side and Mahadevi on the other. Amazed, he watches as an ivory cradle materializes from the depth of the earth. It is a smaller version of the ebony casket. Lying comfortably in it is a newborn. Valakya feels his heart pulse in unison with the babe in the cradle. From nowhere, crimson and cadmium butterflies appear and then disappear into the ebony casket.

That dream startled him awake. Straight backed and cross-legged, he sat on his wooden bed and tied his long, thick braids behind his head. He breathed deeply and focused on his belly, rising and falling, rising and falling. He breathed until the inhalations and exhalations calmed him. For a moment he had felt inner peace.

#

Now in his seventies, Valakya had found solace in the thought that the way one lives is the way one dies. It had taken him many decades to understand that; in that dream of long ago, he was graced with an understanding of the rapture of being alive and the cycles of birth and death.

He lived at the edge of the town in a mud hut roofed with cornhusk thatch. People knew him simply as the sage. Each morning, he strolled to his workplace on an unpaved path flanked by mango trees. Sounds of a waterfall and the rustling of leaves, sap green on one side and copper on the other, greeted him as he entered a clearing sheltered by woven palm leaves supported on four banana trunks. Here, he had arranged his workbench, a storage trunk, and an earthenware vessel with a few cups on the floor. Two wooden stools flanked the trunk.

A piece of mahogany awaited the sage on this summer morning. He closed his eyes, praying to Mahadevi, the source of vigor and vitality. He thanked her for his intuitive abilities and prayed for her guidance in making the image that he had yet to begin. An impression of a figure emerged. He cut, carved, and shaped. His hands and arms, still strong and one with his mind and heart, worked until the sun was at its zenith. He was thirsty. He drank cool water from the earthenware vessel and returned to his work. As he examined what he had done so far, he sensed someone nearby. He turned his head and saw Shankara standing several feet away, waiting for his attention.

"Ah, dear Shankara, what a surprise to see you here! Have you been waiting long?" Valakya placed his chisel and hammer to the side of the roughly shaped mahogany piece. The visitor's crisp cotton kurta was stained with sweat at the armpits.

"No, sir, not long." Shankara wiped sweat from his forehead and stood with his hands folded. "If you could please spare a few moments, I would like to talk to you."

Valakya poured water for his guest and pointed to the stool. "Come, sit here. Tell me, what's on your mind?"

"I don't know if you are aware that I'm very sick." Shankara walked closer and sat down.

Valakya put the cup of water in front of his guest before sitting. Shankara drank the water at once and thanked him. The sage's face dissolved into the sweetest, most loving smile. "Yes, I know, son," he said, his heart filled with compassion. "I was sad when I heard."

"Sir, I have started to make preparations for my final farewell."

"That is a wise thing to do, but have you consulted with the medicine man yet?"

"Yes, I have."

"What does he say?"

"He is not sure, one year or five, 'Only God knows,' he says."

"May your body remain free of pain!" Valakya tenderly patted Shankara's head. The gesture of blessing emboldened Shankara.

"Sir, I have come to ask you for something."

"What is that?"

"I wish to be cremated in a casket."

"Why do you want to be cremated in a casket rather than wrapped in a plain white cotton shroud?"

"I want to leave with pomp and show." Shankara grinned sheepishly. "Would you carve a casket for me?" He looked expectantly at the old sculptor.

Valakya closed his eyes. An image of the ebony casket that he had dreamed of years ago flashed in his mind.

When he opened his eyes, Shankara repeated, "Would you?"

"Yes, son, I will carve a casket for you."

Shankara's perfect row of teeth gleamed against his dark complexion. "Thank you, venerable sir! And there is something else I want to tell you."

"What?"

"I have also asked Bhushan to build me a casket. You know how famous he is and how fond the townspeople are of him. I want to get two caskets made so that I can choose one." He waited for Valakya to object, but the sage did not.

"Will you still make one for me?" Shankara asked anxiously.

"What has my carving a casket for you to do with whether Bhushan makes one or not? Besides, I admire your honesty."

Valakya had not seen Bhushan's work in years. He mused over his own work, comparing his new carvings with the old ones, considering how his style had changed and ripened, and how his work, in turn, had shaped him.

Shankara took a long breath and reverently looked up at the sage. He saw his own reflection in Valakya's tender eyes. His heart seemed to open up.

"I'm afraid, sir, I am very afraid."

"What of?"

"Of dying." Tears welled in his eyes.

"You are human, Shankara. Fear of dying is human, more so in your case."

"Why? Because I am sick?"

"No, because you are young. Most people are afraid to die, afraid of becoming nothing, afraid of the unknown. But an old person who has been awake in life is better prepared to die than a young person."

"Are you not afraid to die?"

"I don't know how I will feel when my time comes. Until then, I try to hone the practice of dying through the little deaths so that I am graceful and openhearted in the face of my own—the Big Death." Valakya put his arm around Shankara's shoulders and gently rubbed his back.

"Little deaths?"

"Yes, the little deaths, children leaving home, separating from people and places we love . . . letting go of unfulfilled desires . . . and the hardest of them all, the death of a loved one . . . all of these are transitions. Transitions are the little deaths, and we must learn to befriend them. They are the stepping stones; they are our teachers."

"Teaching us what?"

"That nothing remains the same. Change, loss, transitions are little deaths between our coming into and our leaving this world. We must learn to let go,

Shankara. Everything is in flux, including our physical selves. The only thing eternal is the spark of wisdom and love in the depths of our being."

"Why don't I feel it?" Shankara asked.

"Most people don't. We arrive empty-handed and leave barefooted. As we grow, we get so busy searching outside ourselves that we forget to look within."

Shankara was listening carefully. He gazed at his feet, mulling over what the sage had said.

After a few minutes of silence, Shankara turned to Valakya and said, "Venerable sage, I don't have time to experience little deaths and nurture the glow in my heart. What should I do?"

For a while, Valakya let the silence surround them. He took in a long breath, exhaled, and felt at ease. His repose also relaxed Shankara.

Valakya said, "Shankara, I know you do not have much time. But I strongly suggest you set some time aside for meditation. Constantly focus on a sacred name, an image or the power within as you breathe in and breathe out. If you learn breathing control, that will alleviate your fears."

"I will do anything you suggest to help reduce my anxiety."

"Find time to sit still in silence every day, preferably first thing in the morning. Do you think you can do that?"

"I will do everything you tell me to do."

"Listen! For at least twenty minutes, sit in solitude and focus on your breath. Watch your belly expand as you inhale and subside as you exhale. In time, you will learn to go within. It will be some time before you feel a difference, son. Have patience. Pay heed. Listen to what it has to say, and you will begin to understand that fear and courage, good and bad, happiness and sadness originate from the same space. When that happens, your own death will not feel as fearful as it feels to you right now. You will feel safe in this space. May you rest in the comfort of that safety!"

"I will follow your instructions. I will take time daily to sit in silence."

"Promise?"

"Yes, I promise, venerable sir!" Shankara thanked the teacher with folded palms and bent head. Then they just sat for a time. Valakya watched the late afternoon sun sieving through the waving palms and the edges of the mango trees. The birds slept. The waterfall gurgled. The sleeve of his robe rustled in the wind. He seemed to have all the time in the world. Nowhere to go. Nothing to do.

"I hesitate to ask you . . . but may I?" Shankara broke the silence.

"Go ahead!"

"Have you experienced moksha, the inner bliss?"

Valakya had lived a contemplative life for years. Under the tutelage of masters, he had diligently practiced the discipline of meditation. He lived in the light of inner silence, the source of all existence.

With a twinkle in his clear eyes he asked, "What do you think?"

"I believe you have," Shankara said, head bowed and hands folded. "I must leave now. Thank you so much for being generous with your time."

Valakya took out a miniature ivory crane from his storage trunk and handed it to Shankara. "Focus on this when you sit still in silence and solitude."

Shankara placed the gift in his pocket, thanked the sage again, and Valakya blessed him. They bid farewell, and the sage went back to his carving.

Bhushan, Valakya's younger competitor, worked in a lavish atelier adjacent to his palatial manor. Townspeople brought their guests to visit the grounds around his workplace. Here, Bhushan displayed a few of his latest works, changing the exhibits frequently. People not only enjoyed his larger-than-life-size works but also liked his muscular physique and handsome face. He charmed them with his almond-shaped eyes and glossy black hair. Underneath his chin, and invisible to most, was a black mole, a blemish in Bhushan's own mind. He habitually scratched it, making it worse.

Bhushan could not understand why the townspeople believed that the work of his senior contemporary embodied spirit. Wasn't his work spirited? He hungered for the repose and peace Valakya naturally exuded.

When Shankara went to Bhushan's atelier and asked him to sculpt a casket for him, Bhushan was pleased.

"It will be my pleasure to carve a casket for you, Shankara," he said. "You are my friend and patron. Why wouldn't I?" He needed to know that he was the only one who Shankara had commissioned to carve the casket. He wanted to make sure that his patron had not asked Valakya as well. When Shankara said he had, Bhushan snapped,

"Why did you ask him?"

"It would not have been prudent of me to ignore him for a commission such as this. Besides, townspeople respect him, Bhushan."

"You know I will carve such a magnificent casket for you that it will glorify you after death—my work will keep your name alive. I see no reason why you needed to ask Valakya."

Shankara cleared his throat. "I asked him, Bhushan . . . I asked him because he is wise and compassionate, and I respect the sage."

Shankara's unexpected answer quieted Bhushan.

As soon as Shankara left, ideas began to flood Bhushan's mind. Day in and day out, he sketched different kinds of caskets from different angles. The more he drew, the more he wanted to draw. He grew ravenous. Some nights, his ideas would awaken him; they demanded to be expressed. One night, he ran a low fever. He got out of his bed, went to his studio, and frantically drew the creatures swarming in his head. The following day, making sketches and then creating three-dimensional models in clay and wood made him feel better. Finally, he selected five designs that could be constructed into magnificent burial boxes. Choosing just one was hard for him to do.

Bhushan could not decide by himself. He summoned his craftsmen and explained his dilemma. "Why not make all five?" his chief craftsman suggested. "Who knows? Shankara might set a trend in the city that could develop into a lucrative business." Bhushan was thrilled with the idea.

The construction began. Each burial box took the shape of a mythological animal: the cosmic guardian's hunting dog, the ether god's bull, the storm god's horse, the wind god's deer, and the fire god's ram. The heavenly animals were to be made in the form of winged creatures, ready to soar toward the blue sky.

Bhushan ordered a variety of woods, ivory, marble, schist, gems, and gold and silver pieces. Based on his drawings, craftsmen began to construct, carve, and stud. Bhushan's other patrons were restless. He had other commissions to attend to, but checked in daily to supervise his best craftsmen working on the five caskets.

Valakya pondered. What sort of earthly vessel would Shankara want to take his final journey? Which casket shape would comfort him, put his mind to rest? Sickness had made Shankara fearful. He had become tender to life. What would a person in such an emotional condition like to be cradled in? By whom?

Valakya tried to imagine an appropriate design. He could no longer work on his mahogany piece. He put that aside to work on it later and contemplated a befitting composition for Shankara's casket. One day in meditation, an image of the cosmic egg emerged, golden in color, followed by the idea of a maternal womb. These were good designs but not entirely satisfactory.

The sage remained focused, imagining, picturing, remembering from the storehouse of his memories. A form suggesting Mahadevi's womb emerged. It was a casket with curved corners and concave walls and lid. Valakya's decision was made. In his imagination, he let its lines refine, its shape define, and its form develop. He was to carve a casket in the form of Mahadevi's womb, a womb chamber.

He began carving the exterior with a beautiful piece of six-foot ebony until he could hear nothing but the sound of cutting and carving. One by one, his senses drew inward. His hands worked in unison with his heart-mind. As the womb casket began to emerge from the block of wood, his face was flushed and his ears pink.

Valakya worked for months on this one piece. As days dissolved into nights and nights reemerged as days, animal and vegetable motifs appeared on the exterior. On the outer walls, lions and elephants roamed a jungle—animal power. On the interior of the lid, visible only to the one lying in the casket, was a white crane, the bird that swims as efficiently as it flies, the celestial bird that links terrestrial and celestial realms.

While the two artists sculpted caskets in two distinct styles and materials, Shankara made an announcement to the townspeople. He said that he wanted to be cremated in a casket carved either by Bhushan or Valakya, as he had commissioned both to carve one for him. When the caskets were completed, they would be displayed on his residential grounds for the public to judge and vote for their favorite. He said he wanted to be cremated in the casket of the people's choice. The cremation ceremony itself, however, would be a family affair. The announcement fanned a wave of excitement throughout the town.

The sun shone brightly on the morning of the show and selection. Champak, mango, and pipal trees adorned the vast grounds surrounding Shankara's mansion. The scents of a bouquet of bougainvillea vines, chrysanthemums, and roses wafted on the breeze. Valakya wheeled his casket onto the mansion's back lawn, preferring it to the front. Two young men helped him place the womb chamber on the display platform.

Valakya strolled toward the freshly mowed and manicured front lawn. He was surprised to see not one but five ostentatious caskets by Bhushan already in place. Shimmering in the morning sun and painted in rainbow colors, the caskets had eyes and wings studded with jewels and gold and silver pieces.

At around ten, the front gate was opened. A river of red, yellow, blue, orange, purple, and white flooded in. Conversing excitedly, the tide of men and women flowed towards the five different displays and surrounded the winged animals, their gaze lost in the blazing colors and structured intricacies. The longer the crowd looked at the winged animals, the louder and more excited they became.

"So many . . . Bhushan has made . . . one . . . two . . . five caskets!" a plump wife in a sari printed with sunflowers said to her lean husband in a white kurta-pajama.

"He needs only one! Is this the time to show off wealth?" the husband whispered. "Look at this red one; it looks like your bridal palanquin!"

"Yes, yes! And look at that one!" The wife pointed at another box and pulled her husband to the next display. They stood in front of the one the wife had pointed out.

"It's mustard yellow! Doesn't it resemble the lacquer cradle we got for our Munna?"

"Yes, it does!" the husband said and turned his head around as if searching for something.

"What are you looking for?"

"Something authentic. Where is Valakya's casket?"

"Someone said his was at the back of the mansion."

"Let's go look at his—the one that expresses a sage's wisdom, not just opulence!" the husband exclaimed.

The couple followed a group of people walking to the back of the house. A crowd surrounded Valakya's womb-coffin. The couple pushed through the people to take a look. People were whispering. Silently, the couple looked at the display. A lull had overcome the group. No one talked. But they all looked intently. Some looked somber, others a bit disappointed.

"This one gives me the creeps!" the wife whispered in her husband's ear. She said she wanted to leave. The couple turned and walked away. Many more followed to return once again to enjoy Bhushan's boxes on the front lawn.

Bhushan's phantasmagoric burial boxes had mesmerized the crowd. The townspeople had walked around the exhibits for an hour and then settled on the chairs facing a makeshift stage where Shankara, his family, and close friends sat.

Shankara's assistant got up and greeted the guests. Some people, still standing, hurried to sit in the remaining chairs. On Shankara's behalf, his assistant thanked the crowd for coming and repeated what they already knew: that their vote, although informal, was important to his boss. That their choice would be his choice. People cheered. It was pertinent that they let their choice be heard. Then he said, "Okay, good people, cheer if you liked Bhushan's caskets!" There was a thunderous applause.

Then, one by one, he asked the audience to cheer for Bhushan's five caskets so that he would know which one to pick. When he mentioned the ram, the fire god's casket, people did not stop clapping.

Once the applause subsided, the assistant cleared his throat and said, "Now it is time to applaud for Valakya's casket. Cheer if you liked his work." This time, the applause was feeble, hesitant. People exchanged glances. A few continued to cheer hoping more would join in. But they hoped in vain.

Shankara's assistant announced the ram casket as the winner. Bhushan's team of workers shouted and jumped up and down. The crowd stood up and clapped louder than before. The assistant sat down.

Bhushan stood and said, "Attention! Attention, please! I would like to heartily thank the venerable Valakya for his creation and also for his personal guidance. Where is he?"

People shouted, "Valakya! Valakya!" Valakya was nowhere to be seen. He was seated on a rock nestled in a wooded area, watching the spectacle from a distance.

Between the cheering and applause, the assistant invited Bhushan onto the stage. People stopped shouting as Shankara bowed down to Bhushan in appreciation. Bhushan hugged his patron. Once again, people cheered.

Within a few months of that memorable day, Bhushan was inundated with work. People from his and neighboring towns not only commissioned caskets but also floats, chests, and display pieces. Money poured in.

The next day of festivities was to be on New Year's Day. A wealthy patron from a neighboring town commissioned Bhushan to make him a float using the same material he had used for Shankara's winning casket. He wanted Bhushan to construct the biggest New Year's float anyone had ever seen. Bhushan was no longer young, and the work was challenging. But it gladdened him to know that Valakya was not even asked.

Even though he had to temporarily move his studio to his patron's town, Bhushan accepted the commission. The work was elaborate and intricate. Bhushan worked nonstop. It took him and his team a month to complete the project. On the last day of work, as Bhushan was standing on the highest platform examining the float and the land around it from a bird's-eye view, he fell to the ground and fractured his pelvic bone. He remained in bed under the care of the medicine man for months but did not fully recuperate. He no longer created sculptures. People were sorry to see him disabled at the peak of his creativity.

A year after Bhushan's tragic accident, Shankara was cremated in the ram casket. At the time of his death, he was in peace.

#

Almost two decades passed. The lush green and copper leaves of the mango trees danced under the setting orange sun that shimmered on the thatched roof of Valakya's mud hut. The "sage-sculptor" had gained people's reverence, but he could no longer hear the waterfall or the birds' chirp or the rustle of the leaves.

Valakya bent his head and stepped out the door. His silver braids and the collar of his long white robe flanked his bearded face. He walked out to fetch flowers for his daily offerings to Mahadevi. When he extended his arm to pluck blossoms from the jasmine tree, a few white butterflies fluttered. He gathered a bunch of flowers in a small bamboo basket and returned to his hut.

Once inside, he noticed that the white silk covering of the womb-casket he had carved years ago had slipped to the floor. He placed the flower basket on a stool and tried to cover the casket with the covering, now yellowed. Suddenly, he felt an urge to sit at the edge of the casket. With his wrinkled fingers he touched its textured surface, felt its chiseled grooves and crevices, and remembered the dream of decades ago that had inspired him to carve the casket at Shankara's request. The expression of his dream in ebony and ivory had eased the dread of his own death.

Valakya was physically tired, yet he felt an ecstasy within. A feeling of joy infused his whole being so much so that he had to sit still. He had a glimpse of himself prostrate in the casket, the crane waiting, welcoming, wooing. Slowly, he opened the lid and stepped into it. He lay down and made himself comfortable. He closed the lid on himself and crossed his arms over his chest. The celestial bird gently unfolded his wings and rose toward paradise. Valakya's eyes were closed as it soared beyond the blue sky.

Bhushan, helped by his wife, walked to Valakya's hut with the townspeople. They came in the evening, with fruit and flowers, to pay their daily respects. But the hut was empty. They searched for the sage in and around the hut and in the grove, but he was nowhere to be found.

Bhushan and his wife returned to the hut. They noticed the yellowed covering of the womb casket lying on the floor. Bhushan picked it up, and as he was about to spread it back over the casket, a pull at his heart prompted him to open it. At first, he hesitated, but he paid heed to the nudge and slightly raised the lid. From the narrow opening crimson and cadmium butterflies fluttered out and flew through the windows and the door toward the spacious blue sky. When he opened it completely, he found the chest empty.

SECRET HEALER

Saras waited until he felt sure that Dhaniram had stopped breathing. He jumped off the bed and ran through the kitchen door. He dashed past the blurry confusion of big and small houses, the water pump, the zigzag street shops—the tea stall, the cobbler, the grocer, the cloth merchant—all shut down for the day. He kept running as the crimson streaks of the setting sun reflected like blood in the whites of his eyes. He ran on the paved road that turned into a narrow mud path flanked by thorny succulents. He ignored the bloody scratches the horny cacti made on his shins and calves.

When he came to the foot of the range of hills, he ran up hill, where young bushes were shadowed beneath large pines and maples. Reaching the bald hilltop, he stopped near a single bare tree. The sun that had blazed the whole day became ash. Heaving and panting, he leaned against the tree trunk, sweat dripping from his forehead and neck, his vest buttons slipping from their worn-out holes to reveal his dark skin.

A cough rattled in his throat; he spat and wiped his mouth. With his sleeve, he pulled back the thick shock of dirty hair from his forehead. His clammy pants, several sizes too big, had not been washed in weeks. He had not bathed in days. He could not rest lest they come after him. He ran down the other side of the hill, lost his balance, and plummeted into a pool of shallow water below. His bruises and cuts smarted.

He dragged himself onto the dry bank and felt a bloody gash on his forehead. His ribs throbbed, but the excruciating pain paled in comparison to the fear in his pounding heart. He raised his head to see if anyone had seen him. Through blurred vision he saw a silhouette approach. Panic struck his soul. He muttered a curse and fell unconscious.

#

The old man carried the boy to a hut and laid him on a charpoy. He pushed the small bedstead close to the warmth of the hearth and sat on the edge to clean the boy's bruises and cuts and dress them with an herbal salve he had concocted. He bandaged the boy's bleeding forehead and wiped his body clean with a solution extracted from marigold pistils. Finally, he covered him with a cotton quilt.

As the old man gazed at the half-conscious boy, pity and affection stirred his heart. What could this boy be running from? He tucked the quilt under the boy's feet and chin and walked out to the porch. There, he laid down on a makeshift charpoy for the night.

Saras floated in and out of consciousness. All night, his head throbbed. His ribs ached. His wounds smarted. He touched the bandages around his head and chest. *Where am I? How long have I been lying here? Who brought me here?*

The morning light filtered through the window. Saras heard the door open and quickly hid his face beneath the quilt.

"Are you awake?" the old man asked.

Does he know? Has he summoned the police?

"What is your name?" The old man stood next to his bed. Saras did not move.

"Would you tell me your name, son?"

Saras shrank underneath the covers and remained still. The old man sat at the edge, on the opposite corner of the charpoy. Saras jerked away from him.

"How can I take care of you if I don't even know your name?"

"Why do you care?"

"Because you were hurt, and I brought you to my home."

With squinted eyes, Saras examined the room—the white walls and mud floor. His arms crossed against his chest, his neck stretched, he turned his head toward the wall.

"Did you dress my wounds?" he asked.

The old man said, "I did."

"And change my clothes?" Saras turned on his side and saw the lush vegetation outside the window. He tried putting his feet on the floor, but the pain made him moan.

"Yes," the old man nodded.

"Why?" he screamed. "Go away!" he said and writhed in pain.

The old man got up at once.

"Ahhhh . . ." Saras whimpered, lay down again, and turned to the other side.

"You are hurting," the old man said. "You should feel better in a few days. Thank God your wounds are not too deep!"

Saras watched the old man leave the room. He had a peaceful face and a gentle voice. Was he pretending to be nice, or was his heart as kind as his voice?

After a while, he re-entered the room with a steel plate laden with food. "I brought you something to eat." He placed the plate next to the bed. "You need to get your strength back," he said and turned to leave.

Suddenly, Saras said, "Who are you?"

"People call me the Healer of Plants," the old man said without turning to look at him. When Saras did not respond, he left the room.

What does this man want from me? Saras tried to raise himself but fell back on his pillow with a whimper. Hunger prompted him to try again. He sat up with a moan, propping himself against the pillow. He picked up the steel glass filled with fresh milk and gulped it down. He placed the plate on his lap, gobbled up morsels of roti mixed with vegetables, and topped it off with hot tea. The sugary tea reminded him of his mother's breakfast brew. Tears welled in his eyes. He slid back down under the quilt and fell asleep.

It seemed ages since Saras awoke to the rooster's cock-a-doodle-doo and followed Baba, his father, to the riverbank. From the bank, he would jump in the Tapti River, wash his body, rinse his mouth, and watch his father offer an ablution to the rising sun. After washing themselves, they would fill two plastic buckets and two vessels—one brass and the other terracotta—with water. On their return, Baba would hang the two heavier buckets at the ends of a long bamboo stick that he balanced on his shoulders while Saras balanced the water-filled vessels on his head. Only recently had Saras begun carrying vessels, sometimes even a third smaller one on top of the other two. Just a year ago, he had only frolic as he walked next to Baba, hitting stones with a stick. Year by year he had been given more responsibilities.

Once back home, Ma served them pan-baked roti and dal with such seasonal vegetables as brinjal, pumpkin, or zucchini that she grew in a small garden patch behind the house. She brewed milk-tea fit for the gods. While they ate, she bundled their midday meal in a cloth napkin—roti, mango pickle, a piece of onion, and green chili. They sipped their tea as she ate her morning meal. The three of them would leave their home at the same time—Saras with Baba to herd cattle and Ma to the river to bathe and wash clothes, pans, and pots.

Every morning, Baba and Saras gathered the cattle from the sheds and pens behind their landlord's homestead. The dust flew as the animals scurried through the wooden fences. The bells around the cows' necks tinkled, and flies danced up and down the buffaloes' noses and backs. Baba led the cattle with a long cane stick and yodeled as they approached the pasture. But those carefree days came to an end when Saras turned thirteen.

One day, as Baba was yodeling, he was seized by a bad cough. Saras held his father and settled him on the ground. Before the cattle had time to scatter, Baba felt better. They continued to walk toward the low purple hills where the pasture was greenest. In bare feet, they walked miles going one way until the sun was at its zenith.

The animals busily grazed and lazily chewed their cud. Baba sat down against the trunk of a mango tree and kept watch. Saras' favorite place was the mango grove. He unknotted the bundle of their midday meal. Another bout of coughing attacked Baba. Saras thumped his back, gave him water to drink, and laid out their lunch. The two ate in silence. When they finished, Saras looked at his father's tired face.

"Why don't you lie down, Baba?"

"I think I should, son."

"I'll watch the cattle from the top of the tree!"

Baba patted him on the back and lay down to rest, and Saras climbed the trunk of a mango tree until it branched. He made himself comfortable there, his legs dangling on either side of a sturdy limb as he plucked a mango and peeled its leathery skin with his teeth. The sour fruit made his mouth salivate. He took a bite, and then another and another, until his mouth felt raw. *In a month or two, the green fruit will turn gold. I will be able to bite into the juicy fruit like a monkey and feast on its sweet flesh.* Imagining this, his chafed mouth watered.

He looked into the distance—the various shades of green expanded and extended into purplish-gray hills against a background of blue. He began to hum a tune. Slowly turning his head he took in the view and dreamed of the days when he would have his own herd of cattle, like Baba. Better still, he would live in the city like Chacha, Baba's brother who visited once a year.

From the ground below, he heard Baba coughing again. Climbing down, he collected as many mangoes as he could fit in the pockets of his short pants for his mother to pickle.

As sunset approached, Saras felt a tinge of sadness. He did not want the day to end. But his father was not well and needed rest. The two walked together until they reached a pond. Baba continued to cough as he waded knee-deep into the shallow water to gather the cattle. When the sun neared the horizon, it was time to yodel the herds back to their pens and sheds.

At supper, Saras watched from the kitchen door as his parents talked in whispers. Baba's cough had subsided. The flames from the hearth glowed and danced on their faces. Ma set out steel plates and filled the steel bowls with dal. She had saved all of the sour mangoes that he'd brought for making hot pickle except for one, which she turned into savory chutney. She rolled out, baked, and served warm roti. She ladled second helpings of simmering dal into their empty bowls. Only then did she eat.

"Sleep well, my son! Tomorrow is the day of merrymaking; it's Krishna's birthday," Ma said before he fell asleep. Saras hoped Baba would feel better so that they could leave early in the morning for the temple as they did each year.

As far back as he could remember this was the only holiday they celebrated away from home, at the Krishna Temple, the pride of the town of Ramnagar.

Very early the next day, Saras was glad to see his parents in a good mood. Dressed in their festival finery, the three of them rode a bus to a stop at the center of Ramnagar, then trekked to the temple. Saras walked in the middle, the swoosh of his mother's starched red and green sari was echoing the rustle of his father's white kurta and pajama. Closer to the temple, they joined the throngs of people who had arrived for the celebrations. Walking in rhythm with the river of people, Saras was focused on passing through the hurrying crowd and taking a look at the images of the Lord Krishna and goddess Radha enshrined in the temple's inner sanctum.

One by one, Baba, Ma, and Saras rang the bell hanging at the temple entrance. As they made their way through the main hall toward the womb chamber, they heard the priest blow the conch. They stood in line until it was their turn to hand in their offering of bananas, a coconut, and a box of sweet laddu to the priest. Closer to the door of the inner chamber, Saras gazed at the images of Krishna and Radha and took a closer look at the blue statue of baby Krishna that had been placed near the feet of the two deities. The priest applied the vermillion tilak to each of their foreheads and gave them a teaspoon of consecrated water to sip. He broke the coconut and removed its creamy pieces, then added them, a banana, and a few laddus to a tray over-laden with offerings from other devotees. The offering thus blessed, the priest returned the rest to Baba. Saras and his parents joined the devotees already seated, facing the inner shrine and singing songs of love and devotion for the baby Krishna. They ate the blessed food—a banana, a piece of coconut, and a laddu each, enjoying the familiar songs. When they finished eating, they joined the chorus.

Late in the afternoon when they arrived home, they savored some more laddu with Ma's brew of sweet tea, as delicious as the tea the old man had prepared for him.

#

The superficial cuts on Saras' body were better in a few days, and the deeper cuts had begun to heal. He watched the old man working in his farm-like garden from early morning until sunset. From the window, he gazed at his savior's profile. He reminded Saras of his uncle who lived in the big city. If Chacha had lived longer, he would have looked like this man, whom people call the Healer of Plants.

Chacha was Baba's younger brother. For years, he had worked in the big city. Once a year, he would stay with Saras' family for a holiday. He was muscular and healthier than Baba, with eyes, nose, and lips that attracted women's attention. Baba often remarked how Saras looked more like Chacha than him.

Chacha dressed like city babus, suited and booted during the day, and in loose pajama and shirt at night. If Saras brought him hot tea holding the cup with his sleeve, Chacha would lovingly rebuke, "*Abe gamdi*, O villager! What is this? Why don't you use a tray?" Or when Saras walked in bare feet, Chacha would call out, "*Abe Gadhe*, O you donkey! Are you a boy or a monkey?"

"Chacha, how can I be a donkey and monkey at the same time?" Saras would argue in good cheer, making his uncle laugh.

Saras enjoyed Chacha's stories the most. They were vivid and wonderful narrations about babus and bibis, the city dwellers he mingled with. He described their fine clothes and fancy footwear and their dining habits and discussions at the dinner table as they enjoyed meals of roasted chicken, goat kabobs, aromatic rice pilaf, syrupy jalebi, and mangoes from Varanasi.

The day after their trip to the Krishna Temple, Baba's health deteriorated. He was unable to keep food or drink down. When Chacha got the news, he came for a surprise visit and was saddened to see Baba cough incessantly. That week, Chacha helped Saras herd the cattle.

Day by day, the family observed Baba's energy diminishing. Chacha could not stay any longer. His job with Dhaniram compelled him to return to the city lest he be fired. After he left, Ma expressed her worry about money to Saras. Without Baba herding the cattle, how were they going to survive? Saras assured her that he could herd the cattle himself. Without a word to his father's employer, as Ma was certain the employer would not hand over such responsibility to a thirteen-year-old, Saras herded the cattle, and day after day brought the animals safely home.

On payday, when Saras went to collect his wages, the employer gave him his father's monthly earnings. He inquired about his father's health, as he had heard he was not keeping well. Saras said he was getting better and would be able to return to work soon. On his way home, Saras met a family acquaintance heading toward his own home.

"So sorry to hear about your Baba," the man said, patting Saras on his head.

"What about my Baba?" Saras halted.

"Ummm! You didn't know!" The neighbor looked confused. "Ummm! Your father was really sick, son!" he muttered.

"He only had a very bad . . ." Saras began, but seeing the expression on his neighbor's face, he stopped in mid-sentence and ran as fast as he could toward home.

Outside his home a crowd had gathered, and he heard cries and moans coming from inside. When he entered, he saw Baba's body laid on the floor and Ma sitting cross-legged next to him. She asked him to pay his last respects to his father. Saras pressed his palms together and bowed down. But then he fell on his father and sobbed on his chest. Chacha, who had been summoned back by a neighbor, picked up Saras, made him sit next to his mother, and covered the body with a white shroud. Saras hugged his mother and cried bitterly.

Before sunset, the cremation services were over. The next day, Chacha performed the last rites in the presence of a priest. Chacha was heartbroken and worried about his nephew and sister-in-law. He suggested that Saras get a job in the city. Otherwise, how was Ma going to pay for the funeral and manage the household?

Saras stood tall and asked his uncle, "What kind of work will I do?"

His hand on Saras' shoulder, Chacha sat down on a charpoy and asked Saras to sit next to him. He looked Saras in the eye. "You can work at my employer's home. He is not the best person to work for, but he is looking for someone to help his wife clean and cook."

Ma stopped darning Saras' socks. "Are you asking him to work as a domestic servant?"

"I don't want to live with a stranger. I don't want to be a servant." Saras squirmed in discomfort.

"What's wrong with serving? You get to live with a nice family, the food is free, and you earn money and save it for your ma."

Ma put her head down on her knees and sobbed. Saras patted his mother's back. She wiped her eyes with the loose end of her sari and said, "Have mercy, Chacha. He is too young!"

"Thirteen!" Saras said with pride.

"Now he works herding cows from dawn to dusk earning a sack of grain and perhaps a five-rupee note per month," Chacha said.

Ma picked up her darning. "That is enough to feed us. God bless Baba's employer—he has agreed to keep him," she said.

"If they gave him half of what they gave my brother, that would have been something, but five rupees!" Chacha said.

"They will; eventually, he will earn more when he is a bit older," Ma said. Sitting beside her, Saras placed his arm around her shoulders.

"How do you plan to pay the debt, hun?" Chacha asked.

"I will find a way. I'll work. We'll work!" Ma insisted.

"As you wish," Chacha said and dropped the subject. That evening, he gave his sister-in-law some cash and returned to the city.

The local grocer knew Saras' family well. Out of sympathy, he hired Ma to grind spices. She was to do her work in a shed behind the store. From dawn to dusk, day after day, she turned the millstone round and round grinding turmeric and ginger root and whole chili peppers into powder, only stopping at lunch for a meager meal.

Even after a year of grueling work, she was only able to pay half of the interest they owed the moneylender. The debt kept increasing. Saras worked as hard as his father had, but he did not receive more money, only more grain. The landlord said he was still too young to do his father's job, although Saras knew he did as much, if not more.

Each evening, Ma came home with her face, arms, and sari covered with powdery dust and smelling of mixed spices. Without bothering to change, she prepared the evening meal, making enough to save for their morning and noon meals the next day. They ate, and then Saras helped her wash clothes and dishes. With each passing day, Ma's eyes darkened and her cheeks hollowed. Lamenting her husband's death and forced to grind spices to pay her debtors, she seemed to be fading away. Finally, exhaustion took over.

One evening, Ma did not return home. Saras waited and waited, imagining all of the awful things that might have happened. Anxious and restless, he could no longer sit and wait. He went to look for her at the grocer's shop where she worked. He found her where he expected—behind the store and under the shed, where the air was filled with the biting scent of spices. She was motionless, her legs played around the grinding stone, her head bent, and her hands fallen from the wooden handle. She was covered with yellow, red, and beige powder. Saras sat on his knees and laid his head on her back, embracing her the only way he could. The warmth of his mother's lap had turned cold.

"Where have you gone, Ma?" he wailed. "Where will I go, what will I do without you? Oh, best mother ever!" He realized he was all-alone and would have to fend for himself.

Chacha arrived for the funeral. With solemnity, he conducted the last rites for his brother's wife as he had done for his brother. He consoled his nephew the best way he knew how by trying to make him laugh. But Saras had forgotten how to laugh as he watched Chacha efficiently take charge of his family affairs. Seeing this made him feel hopeful; there still was someone in the world who cared about him.

Chacha sold what little belongings the hut contained. The money he received was used to pay off the moneylender, and what was left he kept safe for Saras. Three days later, Saras, with a bag on his shoulders, and Chacha dragging a tin trunk went to the bus stop. The sun that had made the green mangoes golden was now searing the narrow paved road. Chacha walked with military strides. The soles of Saras' bare feet—more accustomed to sauntering and galloping through meadows and marshes—burned on the concrete. They rode a bus to the train station. On the railway platform, they sat on Chacha's trunk and waited for the train to arrive. Saras blew on the soles of his feet to soothe their burning as Chacha tenderly caressed his head. Finally, the train arrived and carried them to the city.

#

Under the glare of the sun, in front of a large building, Saras stood behind Chacha as he unlocked the door of a ground floor flat. They entered a dark room with a small window that had been closed since Chacha had left. When Saras' eyes adjusted to the darkness, he found the dwelling smaller than the space in his village home. This was no big city house. It was a dingy room with a cooking corner and a common outhouse at the back. As both of them were hungry, Chacha cooked rice and dal on a kerosene stove. There was no fancy chicken, no goat kabobs.

"Let's eat," his uncle said, "and leave for Lala Dhaniram's home right away. We don't want him to be home when we are there." Hurriedly they ate, and when their hunger was satisfied, they left for Chacha's employer's house. To make the half-hour walk easier for Saras, Chacha gave him his rubber slip-ons that were two sizes too large.

At the end of their walk, they arrived in front of a brick house plastered with yellow paint. It was the biggest house on the street. Under the roof of the front porch, Chacha smoothed his hair, took a deep breath, and knocked at the door. Minutes passed, and no one appeared. He knocked again.

"*Thehro Bhai*! Wait! What is this, so much knocking, knocking? Can't you wait!" a stern voice said. The face of the plump woman who opened the door did not look as stern as her voice sounded. Saras stared at her face and neck, which was adorned with a thick gold chain that shimmered on her tomato-colored sari.

"*Bibi*, Mistress, I brought my nephew to work for you," Chacha said to Dhaniram's wife, his hands folded. Flashing a glance at Saras, he said, "Greet your mistress."

At once, Saras joined his hands. "*Namaskar*, Bibi," he said.

"Too young! Too dirty," she said, scrutinizing Saras from head to toe. "Looks like a villager."

"He is from the village, Bibi. He just lost his mother. But he works like a grown man."

"Does he know how to clean and cook?"

"He is very smart!" Chacha grinned, rubbing Saras' back. "What he doesn't know, he quickly learns, Bibi."

"How much does he expect to be paid?" Saras turned to look at Chacha.

His uncle smiled sheepishly. "Who is asking to be paid? Check him out first. But I'm sure you wouldn't want to pay less than one hundred."

"A hundred rupees!" Bibi said, both hands on her hips.

"He will do what you ask him to do and do it well," Chacha said, almost begging.

Bibi rubbed her chin with two fingers and said, "You want me to pay you or him?"

"I will come to collect his salary. I will put it in savings until he is old enough to manage his own money. But please give him a little monthly pocket money."

"I don't want him running around in the house," Dhaniram's wife declared, and then turning to Saras, she warned, "Keep to the kitchen, all right?"

Saras nodded. But he was not sure what she meant. What was he expected to do in the kitchen all day?

Chacha looked gently upon Saras. "He knows his place. He will stay in the kitchen. He learns fast, Bibi. I am telling you, he is smart . . ." Chacha's voice trailed off.

"Say good-bye to your uncle," Bibi ordered. "Then I'll show you where the kitchen is."

Saras did not want to say good-bye. He did not want Chacha to leave. He turned to his uncle pleadingly, but Chacha gestured for him to follow his mistress. "We will stay in touch. I don't live far away," Chacha whispered to his nephew.

Saras hesitated before giving him a quick hug, holding back tears. In a minute, Chacha was gone.

"Come on! I don't have all day!" Bibi called. He turned and followed her.

Bibi led Saras through a wide corridor, passing two closed doors on the right. The kitchen door was the second on the left. She showed him utensils, ingredients for making tea, spices, vegetables, rice, wheat, and varied dals in plastic boxes with lids. She put some water on to boil, asked Saras to make tea, and left. Saras sat down on the kitchen floor and cried until the bubbling water evaporated by half.

Bibi returned to the kitchen, looked at Saras' face, and asked, "Do you even know how to make tea?" He shook his head. She emptied the overboiled water in the sink, boiled fresh water, and taught him to make tea. She gave him a cup to drink and took one for herself to her room.

When she returned with the empty cup, she handed him a towel, a used bar of soap, an oversized old shirt, pants, and vest. "Wash up thoroughly, dry yourself well, and put on these clothes."

"What should I do with my old clothes?"

"I'd burn them! But if you wish, wash that filth. And hurry up; there is work to be done."

He returned to the kitchen cleaned up, and Bibi pointed to a corner and said, "This is your place. Sit there until Babu comes and whenever you have nothing to do."

After the bath, Saras fell asleep, for the next thing he knew he was lying on the floor in the dark kitchen, cold penetrating the worn-out brown blanket. A fly buzzed noisily and settled on his nose. His stomach was growling. Where was he? What day was it? Then he remembered. He had ridden a train with Chacha, who had brought him here. With an acute pang of separation, he softly called, "Ma! Ma! *Hai* Ma!"

During the following week, Bibi showed Saras how to peel, cut, and cook vegetables, prepare steamed rice, and make dough for roti. He followed her instructions, at first clumsily, but in time learning to assist her. He stirred vegetables, kneaded dough, and rinsed rice for steaming. Bibi did most of the cooking. He washed the dirty dishes and swept and mopped the floor.

Saras was glad to sit down in his corner. It had been a long day. He dozed off. A bombardment of angry words between Bibi and a man awakened him. That must be Babu Dhaniram back home! He had fallen asleep once again after a day of manual work. Growls from his stomach joined the sounds of shouting from the bedroom, one loud, the other shrill. He got up and found a plate set with the food he had helped prepare. He greedily ate everything and went back to sleep on the floor.

Several weeks passed. Saras thought of his uncle before going to sleep and after getting up. One night, thinking of Chacha kept him awake. One moment he was missing him, and the next moment someone was poking him in the ribs. "Wake up! Wake up!" Bibi's grating voice woke him. "You sleep like a pig. What kind of servant are you?"

"Send me a cup of tea," Babu yelled from the bedroom.

Pulled out of his sleep, Saras rubbed his eyes and tried to adjust to the dawning light. He watched Bibi place the kettle on the stovetop. By now, he knew how to brew a good cup of tea.

While waiting for the water to boil, Saras scanned the kitchen. Burnished brass pots with black bottoms were on the bottom shelf. On the upper shelves, plates, pans, and aluminum tumblers were stored. Underneath the counter were sacks of flour and lentils. Plastic boxes lined the floor. He stepped softly into the corridor that separated the bedroom and drawing room from the kitchen and bathroom. At one end, on a plastic rope, hung heaps of folded shawls, quilts, and blankets.

At the end of the corridor, in a glass almirah, a display attracted his attention. On a wooden tray were set a teapot, teacups, and saucers of shiny white material. He gently opened the glass door and touched their glossy surfaces, rich and smooth. It had the feel of the city, and this made his mind wonder what exotic things the other rooms contained. He tiptoed to the door facing him. Through a chink in the wood, he looked at his employers: Babu reading the daily paper, Bibi curled under a sheet with a pillow over her head. He peered through the doorway down the hall and saw two ornate chairs and a third that could seat three people. The chairs were arranged in a circle. In the far corner of the room, he noticed a table with a medley of knickknacks and photographs. On the walls hung family pictures and calendar images of gods and goddesses. The sound of Babu loudly clearing his throat stopped him in his tracks. He ran back to the kitchen. Puffs of steam emerged from the bubbling kettle.

"Oh, Saras! Saaaraas, is the tea ready?" Bibi called from the bedroom.

His heart beat faster. "In a minute, Bibi!" He prepared his fine brew and took two steaming cups to the bedroom.

He gave Bibi who was now sitting up in her bed a cup and handed the other to Babu. For the first time, Saras noticed his employer's skeletal body and birdlike face, the rough skin and long nails on the hands that held the daily paper. "Namaste, Babu!" he said. For a few moments, Babu stared at him with a grin that made Saras uncomfortable. Then he went back to his paper. Saras noticed his feet, his heels on the floor, and his toes in his slippers. Babu nodded without looking at him and continued to read the paper.

Every morning, Bibi was at Babu's beckon call as he bathed and got dressed for work. That day, he was to have breakfast with someone in a restaurant but did not stop giving orders to Bibi until he left the house. She closed the door behind him and looked relieved. "He gives me a headache even before my day begins."

Saras sat on a slab facing the kitchen faucet, scrubbing the breakfast dishes. As the water ran, he gazed at the soiled water flowing out to the open drain through a hole where several mosquitoes buzzed. It reminded him of the herd of cattle drinking water knee-deep at the end of the day. The memory made him homesick.

A slap on his head jolted him out of his remembrance. "Areeee, Baba! I don't pay you for daydreaming, but I do pay for that water. Do you understand?" Bibi poked his shoulder.

Saras quickly withdrew his gaze as he nodded and mumbled a few words. Then he got busy with what he was doing.

Within a few months, Saras had learned to make beds, serve food, and buy groceries. Besides brewing good tea, he cooked vegetable and chicken curries, rolled roti, and put *tadka* in dal. Bibi even taught him how to bargain for vegetables and fruit at the market. Soon he was able to negotiate prices with shopkeepers. He tried his best to be a good servant, so he could not understand why he never pleased his mistress or master.

Another month passed. Saras began to ask Bibi about Chacha's welfare. Did Babu see him every day? Why had he not visited him? Could he go visit him? When he brought up Chacha during the rare moments Bibi talked to him, she either changed the subject or said something like *these days, who has time to visit? If he could, he would. If you go to see him and he is not there, then what would you do?*

When Saras continued to press Bibi, she said that Chacha would show up sooner or later if for nothing else but to collect Saras' salary. That made sense to Saras. He knew Chacha loved him and would appreciate his hard-earned wages. He decided he would give most of his money to him and keep only a portion of it for himself. But was it possible that Chacha was so tied up with his work that he had forgotten his nephew also lived in the city?

At the marketplace early one afternoon, Saras had bargained with vegetable and fruit sellers so well that he couldn't wait to share the good news with Bibi. Instead of entering the house through the kitchen door he usually used, he came through the front room where Bibi and Babu were seated, with the bag of vegetables in one hand and a bucket of milk in the other.

"Oh, you stupid orphan!" Babu barked before Saras could open his mouth.

"You donkey! Look at your dirty feet," Bibi said. Saras felt hurt. He had taken off his sandals outside the door and made sure his feet were clean.

"If you ever enter through this door again, I'll break your legs, understand!" Babu warned.

"Are you a *sahib*?" Bibi said. "Haven't I told you to use the kitchen door, slow brain?"

His enthusiasm deflated by the sarcastic rebukes of his master and mistress, he walked out and re-entered through the kitchen, his shoulders stooped and his head bent. He dropped the bag and bucket on the floor with a thud and cried his heart out. But who was listening?

The following week, Saras had swept all the rooms and was mopping the bedroom floor. He bent to rinse the mop in a bucket filled with phenyl solution, but when he picked up the bucket and tried to straighten himself, he wrenched his back. "Ma!" escaped his mouth. Beads of sweat broke out on his forehead. With his sleeve, he wiped them away and sat on a nearby chair.

"Oh, Babu-Sahib, may I bring you a cup of hot tea!" Bibi said. "When will it sink into your brain that the only place for you to sit is the kitchen floor? Get up from that chair! It is not meant for you!"

As she took a few rupee notes from her purse to pay the milkman, Saras sat staring at her. He tried but could not get up right away.

"You thief! Don't stare at my purse," she cried and pulled the purse strings tight and knotted them twice.

"Bibi, I am not! I can't get up. My back suddenly gave up."

"Don't behave like an old lady. Go sit in the kitchen until you feel better."

Ignoring his pain, Saras forced himself to get up and wobble to the kitchen.

An hour later, Bibi called, "Oye, Saras! Saraaasss! Have you died?" She called again from her bedroom in her grating voice. Saras still did not respond. "Oye! Do you want to become an orphan?" she yelled.

"I am already an orphan, Bibi. You can't make me one!" Though he was in pain, he smiled at his reply and felt good about it. If she said anything in response, he did not heed it.

Late afternoon, just before teatime, Bibi called him to come to her room. He stood near the doorframe. "Have you seen my gold chain?" she asked.

"No, Bibi, I haven't." He was standing against the doorframe.

"Don't lie to me! Who else could have taken it?"

"I don't know." Saras shrugged his shoulders.

"Babu will break each and every bone in your body if you don't tell me the truth."

"I am telling the truth, Bibi. I don't know."

"I'll summon your uncle and send you back with him."

The past ten months had felt like hard labor camp and solitary confinement combined. Saras had begged Bibi and Babu to let him visit Chacha, but they behaved as if he had been sentenced to a lifetime of imprisonment with only a little time of freedom to buy groceries. He could not leave his kitchen cell. Saras wished that Chacha would appear through some miracle. Or that he could visit him. But how?

At that moment, he saw Bibi shaking with anger, walking restlessly to and fro. She cried, "I know you took it! Where could it have gone? Do you want me to call the police?"

From the corner of his eye, he saw her staring at him. He stared back, wishing she would go away, disappear, or fall dead.

Suddenly, Babu appeared. Arriving home half drunk and earlier than usual, he pointed wildly at Bibi. "You! You daughter of a landlord! Throwing gold chains down the drain?" He was holding an almost-empty bottle of liquor in one hand while, with outstretched fingers, raised a muddied gold necklace in the other. "How many times have I told you not to take off your gold chain when you bathe? You forget it. It falls on the bathroom floor and washes out with the water . . . and here it is."

Bibi stood speechless. The chain must have drained along with the water from the bathroom floor to the open drain outside. Babu spouted verbal filth at Bibi. She pushed and shoved her husband to their bedroom and closed the door.

That night, Saras thought about ways to run away if Chacha did not come to get him. He had tried to please his masters, to keep them from physically or verbally abusing him. In the process, he had grown sullen and pallid. As he sulked in self-pity, a plan popped into his mind.

#

A couple of days later, Babu came home in the evening demanding that Bibi fry potato chips for him. At the sight of golden potatoes, the smell tantalized him and his mouth watered. After his masters had eaten their fill, Bibi brought the leftovers to the kitchen and saved them near the stove to supplement their dinner.

Glistening with oil, the fried potatoes enticed Saras. He couldn't resist and ate one. Its taste teased his taste buds, and he ate another and then another. Before he knew it, the plate was empty. As he was wiping his mouth with his shirtsleeve, Bibi appeared at the door.

"What happened to the chips? Did you eat them?"

He did not know what to say. She called Babu to the kitchen to teach Saras a lesson. Babu came, heard what had happened, and slapped Saras hard. Then he dragged him through the kitchen and out of the house bolted the door shut. Saras was locked out, left alone in the dark, cold night. Begging for mercy, he knocked and cried saying he would never do it again. But it was as if his master and mistress were deaf. In the wee morning hours, and only at neighbors' coaxing, did Bibi finally let Saras in.

Back in the kitchen, angry, hurt, and scared, Saras thought that his life as a servant was as inevitable as the sunrise and sunset. Babu would continue to beat him and Bibi would continue to insult and humiliate him. "Where am I to go?" he cried. "What am I to do? I wish I were dead!"

#

The next morning, he awoke to the same hellish life, but in that dark cloud was a streak of light. This was the day when Babu's friends were gathering for the evening. A pleasant sensation rose in his heart as he served tea.

Every few months, Babu's friends came to the house to drink, smoke, talk, laugh, and play cards. Saras had enjoyed watching the men interact. Some of those men had been nice to him, patted his back, smiled at him. Some even secretly put a rupee or two in his pocket.

As soon as the guests arrived, they were served hot tea. He took pride in serving the hot brew that they enjoyed drinking. He heard guests gathering as he strained the sugary, milky tea into the shiny white teapot. He had placed the pot on a tray painted with bright red roses and arranged six shiny white cups and saucers around it. He picked up the tray and scurried to the drawing room. As he was about to enter the door, Babu screamed, "Oyeee, Sarasssss!" and Saras trembled and slipped. The teapot, saucers, and cups smashed to pieces and scattered on the floor. The scalding tea splashed Saras' legs and arms. He got up, his soul knotted in fear, and picked up the shards, trying to salvage the unbroken pieces. Bibi ran to the drawing room and watched in shock. From out of nowhere, Babu came and kicked him, and kicked him again and again.

"Forgive me, Babu, forgive me!" Saras shrieked from a fetal position on the floor, his hands covering his face.

"Forgive you? Yesss! Yesss! I'll forgive you, you son of a pig!"

Babu picked up a cane from a corner of the room and struck Saras with it, blow after blow as Saras begged for forgiveness. Babu's actions shocked the other men, and when Saras' nose started bleeding, Kumar Babu intervened. "Stop hitting him! He has no one in this world, and you know it!"

In the midst of the pain, Saras thought of his uncle. Is Chacha dead? Dhaniram was still focused on hitting. Kishore Babu rebuked, "Let it go, Dhani! Do you want to kill him and get hanged?"

It was only then that Babu stopped. Kishore Babu pulled Dhaniram from the boy and forced him to sit on a chair. He saw Saras' nose dripping blood, his forehead bleeding, and his eyes watering. Kishore Babu asked Bibi to fetch disinfecting lotion, a bandage, and medicated cream.

He led Saras to the kitchen and made him sit on a chair. Saras felt his flesh smart and his bones stiffen. He looked thankfully at the kind man. Kishore Babu squeezed his shoulder and said he would make him well. He tended to his bruises and helped him gulp two white tablets with water. Then he put Saras' worn blanket on his shoulders, patted his head, and told Saras to rest; he then left to join others. Saras tightened the blanket around himself and remembered what Kumar Babu had said. *Has my chacha really gone? Am I an orphan?* Yet, exhausted and with the medication in his bloodstream, he succumbed to sleep.

He dreamt that his mother had kept a full tumbler of hot sugary tea balanced on the side of the hearth. The warmth of the tea spread a queer delight through his body. When he woke up, he was glad that his mother and father were dead because he didn't want them to live in this cruel world. He felt hate surge in his soul—a hatred of which he had not thought himself capable.

#

Several days after the tea incident, Bibi was comparatively calm, and Babu indifferent as usual. The only thought that circled Saras' mind was how to run far away. He remembered the day he had arrived at Chacha's one-room dwelling and the meal his uncle had cooked that sunny afternoon.

Saras heard Bibi snore. She had announced that she was shopping that day but complained of a headache. She must have decided to postpone her outing. Saras gently opened the kitchen door, walked out of the house, and shut it tight behind him. He crossed the lane and walked up the hill. For the first time in almost a year, he walked through the city without a task or errand at hand. The warm rays of the sun massaged his numbed skin and aching body. He looked up and let the sun caress his face and shoulders. He rubbed his arms, hands, and palms and put his palms over his face. He remembered how his mother had massaged him with mustard oil under the morning sun. His eyes welled with tears as blood turned his ears red.

The walk through the bazaar bombarded his senses. There were wafts of open drains and decaying vegetables. Then the pungent smells of spices and meats and the sweet aroma of fruit and pyramids of sweet mithai teased him. Under the full sun, the grocers had arranged fresh vegetables, rainbow-colored dals, white flour, and red chilies. The sights made him forget his misery. The meat seller had threaded skewers with chicken pieces to roast over burning charcoal while his assistant baked tandoori roti and stirred tamarind chickpeas simmering on the coal-burning stove. A plate of fresh lemon wedges, green chili peppers, and red onion slices were ready to decorate lunch platters. A man waited to buy an early lunch. Saras' mouth watered, but he was in a rush to reach his uncle's home.

Huffing and panting, he arrived at Chacha's doorstep and saw it padlocked. Outside the door, on a jute charpoy, sat an elderly man smoking bidi. He was wearing a white dhoti and shirt and a pagadi—an elaborate turban.

"Who are you looking for?" he asked.

"My chacha," Saras said.

"Mehnat Ram?" The man asked, coughing.

Saras nodded. "Yes! Yes, him!"

"Sorry, son, do you not know he died many months back? Poor soul!"

"How? How did he die?"

"Run over by a truck. Poor, poor man!"

So it is true. My chacha is dead!

"What happened to his things?"

"His master, that Lala Dhaniram, took them. He said the man had no relatives alive!"

"Oh, Chacha! Oh, Ma! Oh, Ma!" Saras leaned his back against the door, wailing. He dropped onto his haunches. With his arms around his legs and his head on his knees, he could not stop crying.

The old man stood up, walked through the door into his house, and moments later returned with a lunch thali. Saras was still sobbing.

"Stop crying, son. Here, eat something." Saras looked up and wiped his tear-stained face with the sleeve of his tunic.

"Where are your parents?"

"He was my only relative alive." Saras stood up.

The man pointed to the place next to him on the charpoy, gave Saras a clean rag to wipe his face, and silently watched him eat.

At many times during the last year, Saras had thought of running away, and the only place that had come to his mind was Chacha's home. Where would he go now? He would have to return to the place he had run away from. Babu and Bibi may beat him up, but he did have a place to sleep and food to eat. His heart ached at the decision he had to make. What other choice did he have?

The old man rubbed Saras' back, uttering a few words of solace. Saras cleaned the plate, thanked the man for his concern and for the food, and dragged himself back to the house he hated.

Thoughts of revolt and fury possessed him. If he ran away, they would call the police, bring him back, and treat him more cruelly than before. The root of his tongue was bitter. *I hate you, Dhaniram! I hate you, Bibi! I hate both of you! One day, I'll tear you to bits!*

When he returned, no one was home. He seethed in his misery. Thoughts of revenge continued to race through his head.

Someone kicked at his ribs. Startled, Saras stood up and smelled a waft of stale alcohol. Babu, with a lecherous grin, was bending over him. He squeezed his shoulder, and mumbled to Saras to bring him a cup of tea.

Saras woke up, made tea, and took a cup to the bedroom. As he was setting the cup on Babu's bedside table, Babu turned and said, "C-c-ome heeeere, you . . . little pig! Loook at me!" A red scarf was loosely tied around Babu's neck.

Suddenly, with a lusty grip, Babu grabbed Saras' arm and dragged him onto the bed.

"Come . . . sit here!"

"No . . . Babu! No!" Saras tried to free his arm.

As Saras pushed Babu's hand to let go of his arm, the sheet pulled away and Saras saw Babu's erect penis.

"Let go of me, or I will kill you!" Saras yelled. But Babu seemed possessed by a superhuman strength. He pulled Saras to him, embraced his body, and penetrated him, groaning and moaning. Saras cried in pain.

"You motherfucker! I am going to kill you!" Saras said, revulsion filling his body. The smoldering fire that had lain buried in his heart was ablaze with anger. Babu slumped on his bed and appeared to be unconscious. Saras heard a snore escape his wide-open mouth, and hatred and revenge took hold of him. Babu's nostrils moved with each inhale and exhale. Saras stared at the red scarf loosely wrapped around his neck. He leaped onto Babu's side, unwrapped the scarf, and knotted it tightly around Babu's neck. He squeezed it as tight as he could, and the pressure made Babu's eyes pop open. When Saras pulled it tighter, Babu's eyes grew wider. Saras tightened the knot until Babu's eyes seem to come out of their sockets. Then Saras watched him go limp and motionless. He jumped away from the bed, ran to the kitchen, opened the back door just a crack, and cautiously peeped out. No one was in sight. He slipped out quickly, and like a madman, sprinted towards the hills.

#

A week passed. Even as a shepherd, Saras had not seen a place as serene as where the healer had brought him. Sunlight poured through the window. Feeling better, Saras got up from his bed and wobbled to the door. He stood there watching the old man gardening—planting, replanting, and tending. Saplings of plants, flowers, and herbs were ready for replanting. The old man squatted on the ground, next to a mound of potting soil he had prepared by mixing dirt and cow dung. He filled various sizes of terracotta pots with the mixture and planted a sapling in each.

Saras put on the slippers left for him near the bed and walked to where the old man squatted. His back was toward Saras, and he was wearing a soiled black shirt and pajamas.

Saras stood in front of him.

"You feel good?"

Saras nodded.

"Then sit!" the old man said.

"My name is Saras! I want to tell you something." He kept standing, hesitating to continue with what was on his mind.

"Saras—nice name: swan, the bird that can swim and fly." The old man looked up. "What is it you want to tell me?"

"I want to tell you that I am not the good person you think I am," Saras heard himself say.

"No one is perfect."

"But I have done something really, really bad!"

The old man waited for Saras to continue. But Saras was unable to utter the truth.

"No hurry. Tell me when you are ready."

The old man, his gray hair and beard covered with dirt, looked up. Slowly, a grin appeared on his face. "Have your wounds healed?"

"Yes, they have!"

"Would you like to help me in the garden? Become a gardener?"

"I have never worked in a garden."

"Nothing to it. You can learn," he said. "Are you a hardworking young man?"

"Yes, I am, and I feel fine."

"If you feel so fine, Saras, get to work," he said with kindness in his eyes.

Saras helped him plant the seedlings of flowers and vegetables in various-sized pots. When the work was done, they had filled three dozen or so wooden crates with potted plants. With buds sprouting yellow, orange, and purple, the plants were ready to be sold at the market.

Saras looked around and saw that he was in a valley. The old man's house was at the bottom of a hill, many hills away from the one he had tumbled down. In the distance, the people in the other huts looked like specks. The rustling leaves and chirping birds reminded him of his childhood.

As Saras got used to his new routine, he became acquainted with the women and men who lived in the valley. They welcomed him and expressed joy at the old man's "nephew" visiting him from the city. They said it was nice of Saras to come when the work was heavy and the pots had to be taken to the city to be sold. They brought food to old man's house and told Saras that the old man had not cooked since his wife and teenage son had died on their way back from her parents' home some years ago.

Helping the old man was a refreshing routine for Saras. Overwhelmed by his kindness, one day Saras softly said to him, "Thank you for taking care of me."

The old man nodded and gave him more chores to do: prepare the potting mix, fill more terracotta pots, add bone meal to orchids and daffodils, replant overgrown perennials that stood like a battalion into larger pots. They worked from morning until the sun rose to its zenith and descended in the western horizon. Famished and exhausted, they called it a day, bathed, and shared a meal brought by the neighbors.

They ate in silence. Saras looked around at the well-equipped kitchen that had not been used for years. He stared at the old man eating. He seemed lost in a sad thought, and Saras felt the man's pain as if it was his own.

Gurgling and swooshing sounds pulled Saras from sleep. Soothing sounds of nature salved his anxiety. From the window of his room, he gazed at the swaying branches and the flowing stream in the distance. He went outside and walked in the direction of the stream. The closer he came to the water source, the louder the gurgling and gushing became. From the nearer bank, he saw the surface of the water sparkle. The stream vanished into a pond. Closer to the pond, he noticed herbs and scented bushes with varied colored barks, some brown, some yellow, some cinnamon. He paced next to serpentine vines growing along the edges of the walk. In some places, they entwined around trees; one had wreathed itself around a statue of Rudra—the divine healer. Gorgeously magnificent with luster and richness, the variety of greens shimmered like resplendent gems.

#

Each day, Saras awoke excited to help the old man work in the garden, which was actually as large as a farm. Early one morning, Saras woke up to the sounds of the old man loading crates onto the back of his bullock cart. The crates were filled with the pots they had prepared the previous week.

"Where are you taking them?" Saras asked.

"To the plant warehouse in the city. I also need to buy seeds and fertilizer for the autumn crop," the old man said as he hopped onto the cart. "I'll see you in the evening." The old man grinned and rode toward the city warehouse.

Saras stood motionless as the bullock cart disappeared into the horizon. A chickadee flew above, swishing the leaf-laden branches. *He will hear what I have done and inform the police. They will come to get me. They'll arrest me and put me in jail. They will hang me.*

His legs shaking with fear, Saras sat on the ground. He was tired, tired of running, tired of hiding. He did not want to run away anymore. He sat there for a long time until an idea energized him. He was going to prepare the best meal of his life. He would pour the secret ingredient in all his preparations—his love and admiration for the Healer of Plants. His fear was soon replaced by the act of cooking with care and concentration.

#

Saras heard the bullock cart stop in front of the hut and he ran to the front door. He examined the old man's face.

"Did you sell all the plants?" he asked.

"Yes, I did!"

"And bought all the things you needed?" He kept searching old man's face.

"Yes, I did!" repeated the old man.

"Did you hear anything in the city?" Saras could not resist asking.

"Hear? Like what?"

"I don't know! You are the one who went to the city."

"Nope! Now help me carry these things to the storage shed." He pointed to the burlap sacks he had loaded in the cart. One by one, they carried sacks and bags inside until the cart was empty.

After the work was done, the old man took a bath and finally came to the kitchen. Saras was restlessly waiting for him to sit. He wasn't sure what bad things his savior had heard in the city, and he was eager for him to taste the meal. The old man sat down. "I'm famished," he said. And this kitchen has never smelled this good since I lost my wife and our boy."

"I cooked for you, Baba . . . I cooked for you."

"You did! Bless you! I can't wait to taste the food. Let's eat!"

"But I have to tell you . . . I must tell you . . . I killed a man . . . I killed a man and ran away as fast as . . ." Saras cried. "I wanted to run away from you too, but I am tired, so tired . . ." Saras sobbed.

The old man held Saras in a gentle embrace. Then he patted his back and head, still holding him close to his chest. "You did not kill anyone, Saras! I know you tried, but he was not dead. I inquired and got the whole story. I knew most of it the day I found you. You tried to do what many others wanted to do. Many others are thirsty for his blood. He was caught in the act of doing what he did to you. He was charged and is in prison. You are here safe with me, and no one knows. No one can harm you anymore. Come, let's eat, son." The old man released him from his embrace, held Saras' hand, and led him to the eating space in the kitchen.

Saras was filled with love for the old man. He loved him the way he loved Ma and Baba. He could never love anyone more than the Healer of Plants, the Healer of Men.

AN AMERICAN DIALOGUE

Mamta Kashkari, the sprightly bride-to-be, entered the coffee shop accompanied by her parents. She ordered a strong El Indio blend from Tarrazu. Her mother got a nutty blend from Costa Rica, and her father a robust flavor from Nariño, Colombia. They spotted the wedding planner, Mrs. Weiss, seated in a booth with a half-empty cup of coffee. Her father scooted in next to her and sat facing Mamta and her mother.

After the usual greetings, Mrs. Weiss asked Mamta if she wanted her wedding to be planned like her sister's or if she wanted a more traditional ceremony.

"Can't be one-hundred-percent traditional," her father said. "So much of tradition is bound up with the native land and the people."

"I would have liked a typical Kashmiri ceremony, but now it has to be combined with rites from other religious traditions," Mamta said.

"What she is trying to say is that this ceremony has to be eclectic. A little different from our older daughter Meena's wedding. Mamta's should include only select rites from two different traditions, and not too many," her father again interjected.

Mrs. Weiss wrote something on a lined yellow pad. "For starters," she said, "we could do something like a white canopy, if you wish—like the kind they use in Jewish weddings—and decorate the four poles with wreaths of flowers." She jotted down more notes.

"Yes, yes! I like that very much; I have seen it in pictures," Mamta said. She glanced at her parents, who nodded in agreement.

"That would look very nice over the *vyug*," her mother said.

"Please remind me, what is a *vyug*?" Mrs. Weiss asked.

"It is a cosmic symbol called a mandala in Sanskrit. You must have heard of it; it's drawn on the floor with color powders available at home, yellow turmeric, red chili pepper, green dried mint, and white flour. But these two want it made with fresh flowers," her father said.

"I asked the florist to make it in yellow, peach, and red rose petals," Mamta explained.

Mamta's mother wanted the wedding ceremony to include some traditional rituals such as the *vyug, posh puza*, and *nabad*, crystal candy. Some thirty plus years ago, her own marriage had been performed in the valley of Kashmir according to the Sarasvat Brahmin tradition. On the day of her wedding, her older sister had made a vyug of powdered spices on the floor at the entrance of their home. The soon-to-be-wed couple had stood on the *vyug* after the groom's party arrived. As they stood in the sacred space, her mother had fed *nabad* to the bride and the groom. Standing on auspicious ground and fed sweets, the couple was enveloped with sweetness inside and out.

"And the *vyug* would go well with the *posh puza*—when the guests shower marigold petals on the newlyweds to bless them."

"*Posh puza*—I don't know if I'm saying it right, but it made the guests cry at Meena's wedding. Even the groom's family was touched . . . you know, them being Christian and all . . . it was so beautiful," Mrs. Weiss said, "I cried like a baby."

"Oooh, this is getting exciting! What else? What else?" Mrs. Weiss asked. Mother and daughter looked at each other and began speaking in Kashmiri.

The father turned to the planner. "Before we go ahead with all the details, why don't you tell me how much it is going to cost this time?"

"I will detail out costs by line item, Mr. Kashkari, including the florist, the musicians, the videographer and photographer, hotel rooms, caterers, and all the other details. Just strike out the things you don't want, and I'll either suggest alternatives," she said looking at Mamta and her mother, "or delete them. Whatever you suggest."

"We don't want to delete any of the ceremonies we did at our older daughter's wedding. No!" the mother interrupted and glanced sideways at her husband. "We may add a few more."

"Can we put a stop to this somewhere? Let's keep as many rituals as in the previous wedding, but no more. No more expense! There seems no end to this," the father said, moving uneasily on his seat. His wife stared hard at him.

"Daaddyyy! Let her write down all the things we are discussing, and then you can delete the ones over our budget."

"And then we'll consider your deletions—two against one, Daddy," the wedding planner kidded.

"Who is following the budget? There is no end to this spending," he mumbled to himself.

"Oh no, there's something I completely forgot to ask you!" Mamta said.

"What?"

"We want to find someone who can recite a few verses from the Quran."

"Quran?" Mrs. Weiss' pencil dropped on the pad.

"Yes, I did not get a chance to tell you that my fiancé is a Muslim."

Wide-eyed, the planner repeated, "A Muslim! A Muslim fiancé!" She glanced at the bride-to-be and quickly looked into the eyes of the mother and then the father. Their expressions didn't tell her anything. She picked up her pencil and started to scribble something on the pad.

She looked up and asked, "Where is the groom from?"

"Seychelles," the bride-to-be said.

"I find this very interesting—a Hindu family, one daughter married to a Christian, another daughter is marrying a Muslim . . . very interesting. I don't know if I can find someone; I have never done a Muslim wedding," Mrs. Weiss said thoughtfully.

"Usually only imams recite suras from the Quran," the father said. "But that doesn't matter to us. We are interested in the recitation. We want our guests to hear the lyrical sounds of the suras in Arabic."

"Anyone with a beautiful strong voice can recite; it doesn't have to be an imam," Mamta said. "Do you know someone?"

Tapping her pencil on the pad, the planner said, "You know I'm Jewish."

"Of course we know you're Jewish," the mother said.

The daughter and the father nodded.

"That is not the point. We're asking if you can find an Arabic-speaking reciter," the father said.

"Have you met her fiancé's parents yet? What's his name?" The wedding planner had enjoyed planning the Kashkaris' older daughter's wedding. She had found the in-laws good-hearted and generous. Not a prejudiced bone in their bodies. Although she prided herself on mixing and mingling with people of all religions, no one from her family had married someone belonging to another religion. Her family circle was strictly Jewish.

"His name is Amir Abdullah," the father said.

"Seychelles sounds like a made-up country," she said nervously. "You need to be careful."

"You should check the globe. Seychelles is a group of islands near Madagascar. Are you worried about interacting with the groom's family?" the father asked.

"Oh no! I'm only concerned with the usual problems," Mrs. Weiss replied. "Daily news is filled with nothing but the burning of what had once been called the Fertile Crescent. Terrorist groups who trace their lineage to this geographic area quote the Quran to justify suicide, murder, looting, rape, kidnapping, and as you must know, and the massacre on 9/11! I fear for your family. Have you met them yet?"

"Yes, yes, we have met them; they are good Muslims, we have met them on several occasions," said the father. "When Amir's family visits their son in New York, they also come to Boston to see us. In any case, Mrs. Weiss, you are talking about terrorists, what do Muslims have to do with them? "

"That's a . . . uh . . . that's okay . . . no, it is good! I worry. . . how the minds of young men are being poisoned," said Mrs. Weiss. An awkward silence followed, and Mrs. Weiss gave a silly laugh. "Wait till my husband hears this; he is going to get a kick out of this wedding!" She looked at Mamta, then at the mother and the father.

"Why is that?" Mamta asked.

"Only in America would one find a Hindu family marrying a Muslim immigrant with a Jewish woman as their wedding planner. And if I remember the guest list from your older daughter's wedding, they were so diverse. It seemed like the whole world was celebrating! Only in America!" Mrs. Weiss said, who seemed to delight in diversity, except for her view of Muslims and Islam.

The Kashkari family nodded in agreement.

Realizing that an hour had passed in a flash, the wedding planner said, "Okay then, I'll get back to you next week." They all stood up, said their goodbyes, and left the cafe.

Later that night, Mrs. Weiss called the Kashkari residence. Mamta picked up the receiver. "Hi, Mamta, this is Mrs. Weiss."

"Hi, Mrs. Weiss! Long time no see! What's up?" Mamta was her cheery self.

At first, Mrs. Weiss hesitated, but then said, "Something has come up, dear, and I'm afraid I may not be able to plan your wedding. Please feel free to find someone else."

"No, please! What happened, Mrs. Weiss? We'll be lost without you!" Mamta pleaded.

It was as if Mrs. Weiss didn't even hear her. "I just don't feel right about this. I'd be happy to recommend—" But before she could finish, Mamta hung up.

Mrs. Weiss' decision shocked Mamta. She stood up and paced the room. What was she going to do? She made herself sit down and think. With her hands resting in her lap, she focused on her breath—this was the exercise her mother had taught her to do during frantic moments in her life. When her breath slowed, she recalled how ably and successfully Mrs. Weiss had organized her sister Meena's wedding. Mamta had accompanied her sister and the wedding planner to the florist to decide on a color scheme for flowers, candles, table linens, and so on. The three had tasted the food for the wedding dinner and selected the three-tier cake that was to be decorated with fresh berries. During those months of planning and preparation, both sisters had grown fond of her. Mamta could not imagine finding someone as efficient as Mrs. Weiss.

Having absorbed the news, she went to tell her parents, who were watching the evening news.

"What did she say exactly?" her mother asked.

"She did not refuse outright; she simply said something had come up and she may not be able to plan the wedding. What are we going to do, Mom? Daddy, what do you think?"

"Did she recommend someone else?" her father asked.

"I don't want someone else!" Mamta was on the verge of crying.

"No need to panic! We'll think of something. If she can't do it, she can't do it. We'll find someone better!" he consoled.

"Daddy is right, dear. It is late in the day, but tomorrow we'll search for another—the same way we searched the first time and found her."

Mamta left in a huff and went to her room. She wondered if Mrs. Weiss was making an excuse to just avoid planning the wedding. After all, she was Jewish. Married to a Jew. And several times she had confessed that outside her profession she only mingled within a Jewish circle. But in her work, she came across people of different faiths and from different countries. She had not refused: She had said "maybe." Did this mean that she could be persuaded? Could it be that Mrs. Weiss could not even hear of one of her clients marrying into a religion she was prejudiced against? Even before meeting Amir, had she presumed him to be one of the bad guys she had been watching on the daily news? These days Islam was being identified with terrorism—as if centuries of peaceful and prosperous Islamic reign in various world regions never existed.

Yet Mrs. Weiss was a good-hearted woman. Could a little persuasion change her mind? And how? If Mamta took her to lunch and honestly and respectfully explained how she thought her decision not to plan a Hindu-Muslim wedding was rooted in prejudice and fear, she might change her mind. Mamta would tell Mrs. Weiss how her parents had reacted when she first told them about Amir, and how they reacted when Meena declared her love for Mark. But once they got to know Mark and Amir, they came to love them. She could tell her how she herself felt about Amir when she met him at a mutual friend's New Year's party. But they kept meeting, and in time, she fell in love with this man because he was always kind and considerate. So much so that she decided to spend the rest of her life with him—as an individual, not as a Hindu or Muslim or Indian or American, but as a person.

Mamta's wedding day was a year away. She would not settle for just any planner. She would get Mrs. Weiss back. She believed this deep in her heart. "It is said that when a person completely believes in something, the thought goes out to the universe and triggers the desired results," Mamta's mother consoled her.

A few weeks passed. One weekend, Mrs. Weiss' son, Joshua, came to visit his parents with his friend, Adam. Joshua had met Adam at the conference on World Peace Through Religious Dialogue organized by the University of Chicago. Joshua was a sociology professor, but also interested in the history of religions. He had been intrigued by Adam's presentation, "The Relevance of Moses in the 21st Century." At the end of the question-and-answer session, Joshua introduced himself and asked where he could find Adam's book. There was no book, he said, but there would be one coming soon, "The Significance of the Recitation of the Torah," the subject of his doctoral dissertation. Adam was to present another lecture on that subject the following day.

Joshua attended Adam's second lecture and others presented by scholars from around the country. Most of the panels and papers focused on international understanding through dialogue, discussion, and debate. In order to extend the hand of friendship towards a person of a faith different from your own, most scholars concluded, we must be self-searching and candid, but most importantly, we must not be afraid of one's own vulnerability.

Through the years, Joshua and Adam's friendship deepened. Joshua treated Adam like a brother. Though they had grown close, Adam had never met Mr. and Mrs. Weiss. Both their parents lived in different suburbs of Pittsburgh, more than an hour's drive from each other. The two had just returned from attending their fifth conference when they drove to Joshua's parents' home. They had earlier planned to drive separately from Washington, D.C., but Adam's car broke down. Instead, he hitched a ride with Joshua and spent Friday with Joshua's family before borrowing Josh's car and drive to his parents' house.

The feeling of goodwill and peace from the conference was still with them when they arrived. The two talked while Mr. and Mrs. Weiss listened.

The young men suggested going to dinner and a movie. But on Fridays, Joshua's parents stayed home for a nice Shabbat dinner. His mother had roasted a chicken, made potato kugel, and baked challah bread. Adam said, how could they not stay home to enjoy this meal!

Joshua was excited to show Adam how similar his mother's and Adam's habits were. The four sat in the family room with glasses of merlot and continued to talk about how differences could be overcome through understanding. Mrs. Weiss quoted from the Torah and *Nevi'im*.

At one point, during a lull in the conversation, Mrs. Weiss asked, "Josh, in what way do I remind you of Adam. Do I talk like him?"

Joshua looked confused.

"Remember, on the telephone you said he reminded you of me?"

"Oh yeah!" He smiled and then mimicking his mother's voice, said to Adam, "Tell me, who says 'I honor how we reserve a day of withdrawal and repose for contemplation, enjoyment, and culture'"?

"Who? Me?" He looked puzzled.

"That's what my wife says," Mr. Weiss interjected.

"Now listen to this, Mom!" Joshua cleared his throat and tried to copy Adam's voice, 'One day a week, we must escape the everyday world to add meaning to our lives.'"

"Me! Does Adam also say that, too?" Mrs. Weiss said.

"That surely sounds like you, honey!" Mr. Weiss chuckled.

"Both of them talk like that, Dad! It's amazing! When Adam says, 'Spiritual life decays if we fail to sense the grandeur of eternal time. Twenty-four hours of contemplative pause is important—stop doing, enjoy being.' The similarity is uncanny!"

Mr. Weiss laughed and clapped his hands, causing Mrs. Weiss to blush. Adam added, "God is invisible and immaterial—not divided into millions."

"Exactly!" Mr. Weiss agreed.

Mrs. Weiss was pleased that her husband and son had memorized what she often said.

After dinner that Friday they didn't go to the temple, something they routinely did. And the conversation continued.

"God is an awe-inspiring power!" she said. "Did you know, Adam, that when Moses went up the mountain, God showed himself to a neighboring mountain and it came crashing down, making Moses fall down senseless. Yet God is compassionate and merciful."

"Quite right!" Adam jumped in. "Somehow, we have this misunderstanding that He is a stern and wrathful judge, but that is clearly a misconception. God's compassion and mercy are cited one hundred ninety-two times in the Quran, and his wrath and vengeance have only seventeen references. I believe God is goodness and power, the reason why the material world is good." Adam said it with such pride that it showed in the brightness of his black eyes.

At this point Mrs. Weiss noticed his chiseled good looks. His manners were gentle, his movement elegant, yet he spoke with confidence and determination. She loved this fine young man. If she had a daughter, Mrs. Weiss would have been delighted to have him as her son-in-law.

"I didn't know that Islam and Judaism had any similarities," Mrs. Weiss said.

"Yes, indeed, both are rooted in Abrahamic religion. What I like about these two religions is that the soul's individuality and freedom are not only celebrated, but individuality is emphasized. We believe human existence is a precious opportunity to choose the best life has to offer."

Adam continued talking about the similarities between the faiths of Jewish and Muslim people. "When a Muslim recites *La ilaha illa'llah*, there is no god but God, God referred to is none other than the One God of the Jews, Christians, and Muslims. The God who created the universe, revealed his will to

Abraham and Moses, and whom Jesus called Father and Muhammad Allah."

"Oy vey! The same God? And how do you know so much about Islam?" Mrs. Weiss asked.

"Yes, the same God! I have been studying these religions for over a decade," Adam said. "Besides, I am a Muslim," he answered matter-of-factly.

A silence fell over the room. Joshua and Mr. Weiss watched Mrs. Weiss' face turn pale.

"But your name is Adam," she said.

"It is pronounced differently in Arabic, but in English, it is spelled the same," he answered.

Coldness descended upon the room. For the rest of the evening, Mrs. Weiss was civil but didn't say much.

Very early Saturday morning, Adam left in Joshua's car before Mr. and Mrs. Weiss were awake. He would come back Sunday morning, when they would drive back to Washington.

Later, when the Weiss family gathered at the kitchen table for breakfast, Joshua told his parents Adam had left early to meet his own parents for breakfast.

"Nice young man!" Mr. Weiss said.

"Josh, why didn't you tell me your friend was a Muslim? I had no time to mentally prepare myself." Mrs. Weiss was upset, her eyelids puffy.

"Why did you need to prepare?" he said, pressing his lips together.

She lowered her eyes and took a deep breath.

"Let me ask you something, Mom," Josh said. "What right do we have to shut ourselves off from people simply because they belong to a different religion?"

"No right! We meet people all the time. If we like them, we extend the hand of friendship. If we don't, we keep our distance," she said.

"She is not against anyone, Josh. She gives everyone space," his father said.

"Except if he happens to be a Muslim." Josh retorted.

"Why drag misery home?" his mother said.

"That's what I am talking about. Was Adam miserable? There are many people we know well—talk about misery!" Josh snickered. "I thought you were open-minded, different from the rest of our family, even more liberated than Dad. With a friend like Adam, my life is richer, Mom. Since he became my friend, I have met people from different parts of the world. I thought you too felt that about your clients. But it seems to be otherwise," he said, nervously tapping his leg against his chair.

In her community, Mrs. Weiss was regarded as a good-hearted and open-minded woman—accepting of other people. After all, she had planned weddings for Hindu and Christian families. But mingling with Muslims? That was emotionally too hard.

Joshua refilled his coffee cup and went out to the porch; his father followed. As Mrs. Weiss sat at the kitchen table, she heard the men she loved dearly talking and laughing. She preferred sitting alone; her heart was heavy. Someone rang the doorbell, disturbing her thoughts. At the front door stood a police officer.

"Hello?" she said.

"My name is Officer David Mallick, ma'am. Is this the Weiss residence?"

"Yes, it is?"

"Does Joshua Weiss live here, ma'am."

"Yes, he is my son. He is here."

"Was someone else driving his car then?"

"Wait a minute, please! Why don't you talk to him?" Mrs. Weiss' hands were shaking, "Josh!" she called. "Come here! Who is driving your car? This police officer wants to talk to you."

Joshua could hardly speak when he informed his parents that Adam, who had borrowed his car, was killed in an accident. He left with the police officer to identify his body.

Mrs. Weiss, shocked to hear the tragic news, found herself heartbroken. When the two men left, she thought about how, through a short encounter with this fine young man, she had unwittingly crossed an ocean. She had come one step closer to a faith she feared she would never accept. She had not known the immensity of her prejudice until Mamta mentioned her fiancé's religion. How was she to combat her darkness?

Hadn't she had similar thoughts about Hindus before she met the Kashkari family? Yet they turned out to be a lovable family. And their daughter's wedding celebration was lovely. Because of that one family, she had grown fond of Hindus. Adam had said the way to embrace differences was by being open, vulnerable, and candid. Was she being given an opportunity to look closer at individuals and not judge an entire group by the behavior of a few fanatics?

The memorial service for Adam was to be held in a mosque in Monroeville, where Adam's parents lived. Joshua suggested his parents attend. It would make them feel better. Since the accident, Mrs. Weiss had not been herself. But something in her said in order to heal, she must attend. Besides, Mr. Weiss insisted that she consider going.

As they entered the front gate, they were led to separate sections—Joshua and his father with the men and Mrs. Weiss with the women. Sounds of laments and sobs echoed in the silence. The imam, an older man with white hair and beard, stood in the middle facing the gathering. In his thunderous voice, he began to recite in Arabic, a language she had never heard. Mrs. Weiss was fidgety. She did not know what to do or how long it would take for the recitation to be over. With a questioning glance, she turned to the woman on her left who was wearing a sky-blue-and-white hijab. "He is reading *fatiha*, the first verse from the Holy Quran," the woman said. Mrs. Weiss faced the front and tried closing her eyes in order to concentrate. But to no avail. She turned to her right. A woman with a purple scarf tied around her head smiled and took out a white handkerchief from her handbag and offered it to Mrs. Weiss, gesturing for her to place it on her head. Reluctantly, Mrs. Weiss placed it over her hair and whispered, "Thank you!"

The collective focus of the gathered people was on the recitation. So she too closed her eyes. In the darkness, Adam's face appeared. She sighed, remembering his elegant manners and the motherly feelings he had aroused in her. The sounds of Arabic words streamed through her, replacing Adam's memory, his image dissolving into the phonic sounds of the imam's thunderous voice. The recitation of the verses had a soothing effect. She focused on the melodic sounds. When they stopped, she opened her eyes and saw the imam move back several steps. A young man took his place and introduced himself as Irfat Salaam. A minute's silence in the space ushered in a serenity that affected all.

Dressed in white pajama and shirt, Irfat said he would recite verses of the Sufi poet, Rumi, in English. A calm had overcome Mrs. Weiss. She became attentive.

"I will be with you in the grave on the night you leave behind your shop and your family." The young man's words were like pearls in a necklace. "When you hear my soft voice echoing in your tomb, you will realize that you were never hidden from my eyes. I am the pure awareness within your heart, with you during joy and celebration, suffering and despair." She thought of Adam. The feelings he had left behind were still with her.

"Do not see me through haze, see me clearly, see my beauty without the old eyes of delusion." Was he talking of the kingdom of God within? She understood the language of the poet.

The young man continued, "What kind of gossip-house have you opened in our city? Close your lips and shine on the world like loving sunlight." Mrs. Weiss felt as though Rumi were talking directly to her. So what if he was a Muslim? Her eyes welled with tears. She pulled the handkerchief from her head and wiped her eyes. The two women flanking her turned their heads, but seeing what she was doing, turned back to Irfat Salaam.

Mrs. Weiss was lost in thought during the hour-drive home. As soon as they arrived, Joshua asked, "Mom, may I help you prepare lunch?"

"Thanks, Josh. But first I have to make a phone call."

For the past month, Mamta had been surfing the web in search of a new wedding planner. She was reading newlyweds' comments about a wedding planner when her cell phone rang. It was Mrs. Weiss!

"I'm sorry, dear, for what I said to you last time I talked to you! I wanted to let you know that I'm available to plan your wedding to Amir Abdullah. That is if you have not yet found a planner, and if you would still let me?"

GAURI'S FREEDOM

Only three months ago, Gauri was in her studio putting finishing touches to the last oil painting for her debut show. It had been two years since her graduation from art school. She had passed with flying colors and returned home to live with her parents and work towards her first solo exhibition. She had booked a gallery and created twenty-one paintings, and the show had opened to great reviews. But what followed for months after the show happened so fast that Gauri felt she was watching someone else's life fly by.

Bansi Pandit, the matchmaker, had come to Gauri's home with a marriage proposal. He had found a suitable boy for her. His name was Ramji Raina, from a well-respected family originally from the valley of Kashmir. Ramji was an architect turned businessman. A self-made man, he managed a successful business importing Kashmiri jewelry, clothing, and crafts to the United States, where he now lived.

"He lives in Amreekah?" asked Gauri's mother, Maji, who sat next to her husband.

"Yes, Amreekah! If he agrees to this match, she'd be a lucky girl!" Bansi said.

"What about his family? Where do they live?" Gauri's father, Molaji, said.

"They live in Amreekah. Here! Here in this mansion." The matchmaker pointed to a photograph that he had pulled from a worn brown leather folder and handed it to Molaji. He held the picture so that his wife could also take a good look at it. They nodded in unison, exchanged smiles, and passed it to Gauri. A handsome man in gray pants and a herringbone jacket stood in a garden in front of a Tudor brick house, partly obscuring a bay window. It definitely was not love at first sight, she thought, but what can one know about someone from a photograph? She handed the picture back to the matchmaker.

"You can keep that, Gauri!" he said. Gauri gave it to her mother.

"He is an only son," the matchmaker said. "Your daughter will reign like a queen in his home." He looked at Gauri. "How fortunate is that, *kuri*!" He continued to sell the Raina family on Ramji, telling them how he would make the kind of husband women pray for and be the son-in-law parents dream about.

"No demands from his parents?" Maji asked.

"No dowry, no demand—and listen to this! He only requires that the girl is educated and does not want to work outside the home."

"Our daughter works at home," Maji said.

"Once or twice a year, she goes out to show her paintings at art galleries—that's all," her father added.

"Who wouldn't want that!" the matchmaker said.

Gauri had nothing against an arranged marriage. But she wanted a simple ceremony. Why waste money on an elaborate traditional affair? She could use that money to buy art materials. She had thought about such things as her parents searched for an eligible boy for her. They suggested a few fine matches; some young, some middle-aged, even one widower. But after listening to them talk to her parents and then her, Gauri felt they were neither interested in art nor ready to live the rest of their lives with an artist. Some of them didn't even understand what the big deal was about art. Imagine that! Her parents were patient, waiting for her to say yes to any of them—except the widower.

When she looked at Ramji's picture for the first time, she saw that he was handsome and dressed impeccably, standing in front of a beautiful house in a flower-laden garden. Something inside told her that he would have an appreciation for art and her vocation. If she could meet and talk with him, she could decide if she wanted to spend the rest of her life with him. She told her parents this after the matchmaker left, and her parents agreed.

The following week, Molaji and Maji investigated the Raina family's background, only to hear good things. The young man lived with his parents in the United States, where he had prospered and made a good life for himself. He was an obedient son and would likely make a good husband.

Ramji had come to the valley for a two-week visit, during which time he had hoped to find a young woman to marry. It was his third trip for this purpose. His parents had accompanied him during his previous visits, but this time they stayed home in Pittsburgh, Pennsylvania. The matchmaker took Ramji to see other eligible young women. He charged his clients based on their income: the richer the client, the higher the commission. He took Ramji first to the homes where he could expect better payment for his services. He brought Ramji to Gauri's home just a few days before he was to fly back to the States. A hurried arrangement for an evening tea was made, and at the door, Maji and Molaji received them.

After tea, Gauri and Ramji were left alone in the room. For several hours, they talked about art, Ramji's handicraft business, and Gauri's love of painting. She showed him some of her favorite pieces, and he appreciated her skill. He was charming, and she liked him. He must have liked her too, because he wanted to marry her.

Two days later, a simple wedding ceremony was performed. That night, Gauri and Ramji shared a bed. Gauri turned away from Ramji. Intermittently through the night she wept, thinking of the eight thousand miles that would separate her from her parents once she landed in the United States.

The day after the wedding, Mr. Ramji Raina and Mrs. Gauri Raina took three connecting flights, spending eighteen hours on planes and several hours at airports. They finally reached Ramji's brick Tudor house at 2 a.m.

They stood on the threshold of the Rainas' five-bedroom mansion. In the surrounding darkness, the lighted front door welcomed them. Ramji's mother, Ammaji, opened the door. Behind her, Ramji's father, Boji, greeted them with a smile and hugs. Ammaji looked at Gauri, from her ponytail to her Nike sneakers, and said, "Welcome, *bahu*, daughter-in-law! You already look like an Amreekan!"

"Welcome home and congratulations, son and daughter-in-law!" Boji said as Ammaji circled a water-filled brass vessel three times in front of the newlyweds and three times over their heads.

"Eat this," she said, putting a piece of rock candy into Ramji's mouth, and then she offered the candy to Gauri. "You too! May your life be as sweet as this piece of *nabad*!" She kissed them on their foreheads, concluding the welcoming ritual. Boji hugged his son, patted Gauri's back, and led them through the foyer to the family room.

In the bright indoor light, Gauri admired Ammaji's silk salwar kameez, with a design of red, yellow, and blue flowers. Her head was covered with a matching georgette chunni as she served hot tea and syrupy jalebi and yellow ladoo and pistachio burfi.

"Eat something!" she said to Gauri. After the longest flight of her life, the jet lag was affecting Gauri. She could not eat a bite. She said so to her husband's mother, and added that the tea made her feel better.

"Sweets are auspicious, *bahu*. You must take a bite!" Ammaji said, and put a piece of jalebi on the saucer that held Gauri's teacup. She left it untouched. But Ramji ate jalebi and burfi with two cups of tea as he described to his parents the details of the quick wedding and the few guests he had invited and most of those who attended. Ammaji inquired about the health of all their relatives and friends.

"Go to sleep before it is sunrise!" Boji interrupted. "You must be exhausted. We'll talk tomorrow."

"Yes, go rest! No need to get up early tomorrow!" Ammaji said. Gauri bid *namaskar* to her newly acquired in-laws. After the parents retired to their bedroom, Ramji led Gauri to his bedroom on the second floor of the house, where the other bedrooms were. His room was impeccably clean, but its walls were stark. The bed felt comfortable. The curtains were drawn over a large window. This was going to be Gauri's new home. This was where she was going to spend her first night in America. This was where she was going to spend the rest of her life with Ramji.

In the morning, Gauri opened her eyes to unfamiliar surroundings. The strange sounds and smells made her sit up abruptly. Her body had not yet adjusted to the ten-hour time difference. So as not to wake her sleeping husband, she put her henna-painted palm on her right wrist and held her gold and red glass bangles to keep them from jingling. Her cheeks flushed as she thought about the previous night with her groom. What they had done was natural, an ordinary act between a husband and wife. She slid to the edge of the bed, straightened her legs, and stretched her feet to look at the intricate henna designs on them. But the light streaming through the window obscured the patterns. The view of the front garden from the bay window, partly hidden, was so foreign, so different than the river view from her father's study, which she had shared with him for her studio. Molaji had let her set up her art studio on the side of his study where floor-to-ceiling glass windows had better light and a beautiful view of the River Jehlum. From the time she was nine, she had drawn the flowing river at various times of the day, more times than she could count.

Her debut art show displayed paintings of the distant lower Himalayan ranges; the skyline of the houses on the opposite shore; the floating shikara boats, curtained and cushioned for tourists; and plain wooden boats that vendors used to sell lotus roots, mauve-colored *brinjal*, cherries, green walnuts, and other luscious fruit and vegetables. She had also painted views of the riverfront at sunrise and under a full moon, fishmongers gutting fresh catches, washer men cleaning clothes, women balancing water pots on their heads, and the grapevines that grew in the central patch of garden that separated her studio from the main house.

With her fingers crossed, Gauri would turn until she found a view she liked. Then she transformed the three-dimensional scene of her liking into a two-dimensional composition on canvas that she stretched and gessoed herself. Their sizes ranged from four-by-seven to five-by-six feet—taller and bigger than the painter.

In the studio, Gauri had felt comfortable surrounded by her drawing books and pads, paintbrushes, tubes of oil paints, and bottles of turpentine and linseed oils. She had painted every day, standing in front of her easel facing the river. She painted after breakfast until her mother called for lunch and then again until teatime. Under the easel, Maji spread an old rug. She had not wanted the walnut floor to get splashed with viridian and sap green, cerulean and ultramarine blue, alizarin crimson and cadmium red the way Gauri's t-shirt and jeans were splashed and spotted.

In Ramji's bedroom, under the windowsill of the bay window, they had piled their luggage: suitcases, her duffel bag, and the bundle of her sketches and drawings that Maji had helped her pack. Gauri walked softly closer to the window and stared out. A large weeping willow shadowed the front of the house. Its green branches swayed gently in the spring wind, the rising sun shining yellow through them. A robin perched on one of its branches, singing sweet and shrill.

Holding onto the bangles, Gauri walked to the bathroom before letting them go. Ramji's bathroom was as big as her bedroom had been in her parent's home. It had white and mauve tiles. Last night, behind that curtain, she had discovered a white tub. "Am I to take a bath in this thing?" she had asked Ramji. He nodded, saying that if it was too big, they could bathe together. Her face flushed thinking of that. He also said one of the two sinks facing the mirrored wall was for her to use. A sink to herself—this was luxury.

Scented soap on an oval china plate sat beside the faucet. A matching tooth glass stood next to it. Gauri splashed some water on her face, patted it dry, and brushed her teeth. As she combed her waist-length black hair, she looked at her reflection in the mirror. The face looked unfamiliar. Who was she? Gauri! Yes or no, she could not decide. Maji had said she belonged to her husband and his family now. Gauri had said she knew nothing about the Raina family, to which her mother had said it would take time for her to get to know them. At least a few months to observe how they thought, talked, behaved, what they believed, and then adjust and live accordingly.

"You are smart and well-mannered; you will know how to carve out your space without much effort. Try not to displease anyone," Maji had said.

Having combed her hair, Gauri knotted it in a low bun. She moved the gray and purple striped curtain that hung over the bathroom window to one side and glimpsed the red, white, and blue American flag gently fluttering at the end of a pole. The rigidity of the pole and the rippling of the flag struck her. It stood in front of a brick house. With a stone pathway and green grass on both sides, the view inspired a cityscape in Gauri's mind. She couldn't wait to sketch it, paint it. She couldn't wait to buy colors and brushes and canvas to paint that scene.

She returned to the room and saw Ramji sleeping like an angel. The matchmaker was right. She was indeed fortunate to find a husband like him. When he woke up, she was going to announce the subject of her painting. The thought excited her. She jumped onto the bed, waking up Ramji with the jingle-jangle of her bangles.

"You are up already? Come to bed!" he groaned, his eyes still closed.

"Not now!" Gauri said.

"Then why did you wake me up?" He turned toward her.

"I want to tell you something," she said.

"What?"

"I know what I want to make for my first painting in America! Do you want to see?" she said excitedly.

"See?" He had not yet opened his eyes.

"Come to the bathroom. You can see it from the bathroom window."

"Later, I'll see it later when I go in there. Right now, I want you to come to bed." He pulled her onto his chest and leant his head on the pillow against the headboard. His eyes fell on his desk clock. "Oh shit! I've a meeting at nine!"

Like a fox, he leapt from the bed, tossed his nightshirt to one side, dropped his pajama pants on the floor, and walked out of them, leaving them there.

"Help me get dressed!"

"Help you dress? Why?"

"Please, Gauri, get my clothes!" he said impatiently and rushed to the bathroom. He hummed a tune as he showered.

"Where do you keep your clothes?" she called.

"Second door to your right."

What Gauri saw behind the second door to the right astounded her. She stared open mouth at the walk-in closet that looked like a men's clothing store. Shirts and trousers, jackets and coats, ties and bow-ties were hanging on a rod. T-shirts and casual pants were neatly folded and stacked on shelves from the lightest to the darkest color. Underpants and undershirts, socks and handkerchiefs, sweaters, scarves, and gloves were placed in neat piles. In that symmetry and order, she sensed coldness. She hesitated to pull out something lest she disturb the order. When she heard Ramji call her name, she snapped back to attention. Randomly, she pulled out a blue shirt and a pair of black pants. She closed the closet door behind her, walked to the bathroom, and hung the clothes she had picked inside the door.

"Gauri, my underclothes?" Ramji said, standing in the doorway, a bath towel wrapped around his waist.

She returned to the closet, picked up briefs and an undershirt as if she were handling delicate china, a pair of black socks, and a white handkerchief from their respective piles. She handed the underclothes to him and left the rest of clothing on the chair next to where he was standing. She shot him a questioning look.

"What?" he said. "I am used to Ammaji doing these things for me. She can still do this if you don't want to! Do you mind?" he said.

It took her a few moments before she said, "I don't mind this once, but from now on, you'll have to do it yourself! Now get dressed!"

While Ramji dressed, Gauri picked up his discarded nightshirt and pajamas and folded them. As she did, her glance fell on the roll of her paintings lying on top of her suitcase. She began to make the bed.

"I hear your mother in the kitchen. I should go down and help her," Gauri said, and Ramji nodded in agreement.

As Gauri walked into the kitchen, the sweet aroma of Kashmiri chai and crushed cinnamon and cardamom reminded her of her own mother in her kitchen and the temple bells calling devotees to the first worship of the day.

Boji was sitting quietly at the kitchen table, waiting for his breakfast. Ammaji had her back toward the kitchen door, pouring tea for him. Gauri, a bit self-conscious, greeted both. "What can I do, Ammaji?" she said.

Ammaji pointed to a pile of plates and cutlery. A stack of fried paranthas and a large omelet had already been made. "If you don't mind, set the table, and I will serve." Gauri did as she was told.

Ramji came down hurriedly and greeted his parents; they blessed him. He sat next to his father, who asked if he felt jet-lagged, why he was up so early, and most importantly, "Why don't you take your bride out instead of going to some meeting?" Ramji explained that there was no way he could miss the meeting that had been planned long before he left for India with a businessman named Sukumar Sen. He was semi-retired and captivated by Ramji's art-and-craft stores. He wanted to invest in the business, consolidate it into a company, and become his partner. Ramji did not want to cancel their first meeting and create a bad impression.

Ramji gobbled the omelet and *parantha* with swigs of tea. He accidently dropped his fork but didn't bother to pick it up, wiped his face with a napkin, tossed it to the center of the table, then left. Boji ate leisurely. After he had eaten, he hid behind the *Pittsburgh Post-Gazette*, only his hand creeping out to pick up a fresh cup of tea. After the men were finished eating, Ammaji served herself and Gauri. The two women ate quietly; Gauri was too jet-lagged to initiate a conversation. She stared alternately at her food and out through the window. When they put the dirty dishes in the washer and swept and mopped the kitchen floor, Gauri thought the kitchen work was done. But Ammaji busily rinsed collard greens and asked Gauri to measure a cup of basmati rice into a pot and rinse it to cook for lunch. Then they dusted and cleaned the house and washed a load of laundry. After a lunch of rice, greens, and buttermilk,

Ammaji said it was time for a siesta. Gauri was glad to go to her room and rest. But before she felt rested fully, Ammaji woke her up at teatime. Gauri forced herself awake. Ramji came home after they had finished tea. Excited, he gave them the news about signing a contract with Sukumar Sen. They chatted a little as Ammaji cut cauliflower while lamb for rogan josh simmered on the gas stove for dinner. Gauri cleared the teacups from the table thinking, where did the day go?

The next day after breakfast, Gauri asked Ammaji, "Do you mind if I unpack now?"

Ammaji looked at her with raised eyebrows. "Didn't you unpack yet?"

Gauri, a little surprised, shook her head.

"Then go, hurry up and unpack. God knows where those bags have been! We need to clean your room. It has not been cleaned in two days!"

Gauri's heart was heavy. Clean the room? The spotless one? She entered her room with its gleaming windows and fluffy rug and walked to the corner where Ramji had pushed her roll of drawings, suitcase, and duffel bag. She unzipped the suitcase first. A lingering aroma reminded her of home, and she burst into tears. The unfamiliarity of her foreign surroundings intensified the feelings of loneliness, separation, and being so far from Maji and Molaji.

She took out the drawing book and turned over the front cover. On the first page was inscribed: *To our dearest daughter, Gauri. Fill this book with new scenes and sights that inspire you in America. Molaji and Maji.* She touched the names of her parents with her fingertips. Her eyes moistened as she imagined their faces. On the reverse side of the front cover her father had taped a red envelope—she had forgotten it was there. Inside the envelope were five hundred dollars. She remembered the day when Molaji had gone to the bank and brought the American currency home. When Maji had looked at him with questioning eyes, he said, "Just in case!"

"Just in case of what?" She asked as he taped the enveloped inside Gauri's drawing book.

"Maybe nothing, maybe something, you never know," he'd said.

Maji had rolled and tied Gauri's three landscapes and a few other drawings with a piece of hand-spun rope. Gauri's slim fingers worked at the knot; she untied, unfurled, and unwrapped the roll to flatten them.

In the walk-in closet, Ramji had emptied some closet space and two shelves for her to use. She neatly stacked her colored petticoats, blouses, and underclothes on the shelves. One by one, she hung her saris of every texture and color, brocaded with gold and silver threads, on hangers. Silk saris were soft and thick, and tissue saris transparent, but most had tassels knotted along the edges. At one end, she hung a few pairs of jeans and the t-shirt in which she had travelled. A vanity with a full-length mirror was just outside the closet door. She placed the red velvet box that contained her gold and silver jewelry sets along with the money-filled envelope in the upper drawer. Carefully, she slipped her artwork facedown into the large bottom drawer.

"Are you done? I'm ready!" Ammaji's voice startled Gauri. Holding the vacuum cleaner with one hand and the other on her hip, she stood at the door, instructing Gauri to carry the empty suitcases downstairs. Then she got busy cleaning.

Later in the kitchen, Ammaji fluffed the steaming rice. The suitcases were still at the bottom of the stairs. Gauri asked, "Ammaji, where should I put the suitcases?"

"In the basement."

But before Gauri could carry them down into the basement, Ammaji said, "On second thought, it's better if I take them myself. You wouldn't know where to put them. Just take them to the bottom of the basement staircase and leave them there." Gauri shrugged her shoulders and did as Ammaji had instructed.

#

Two months passed. Gauri fell into the daily routine of cooking, cleaning, washing, and other domestic chores. It was as if she had come to America to assist Ammaji during the day and be with Ramji during the night. With her oiled, silver-streaked hair pulled tightly into a chignon and dressed in a faded salwar kameez, Ammaji pulled the furniture away from the walls. She dusted the cushions, vacuumed the carpets, and bumped Gauri out of the way. Gauri was given the task of dusting the furniture and cleaning the windows and doors. After Ammaji finished vacuuming, Gauri mopped the floor not covered by carpet. When everything was cleaned, the carpets were unrolled and the furniture moved back onto the dents already there. Cushions were arranged precisely, objects that had been moved, even a little bit, were readjusted. All this was done while listening to popular Bollywood tunes or devotional songs.

The work of washing and drying a small load of towels, underclothes, and linen was Gauri's responsibility. Whenever Ammaji saw the basket of folded clothes, she frowned. Most days, she had other things to do, but one day, when Gauri was carrying the basket loaded with clothes, Ammaji said, "Are those folded?"

"Yes." *Why would she even ask,* Gauri thought. *Of course they're folded.*

"Let me check!" Ammaji snatched the basket away, checked a few layers and mumbled, "No, no, no!" Then made Gauri sit next to her. She turned the basket upside down. "Watch and learn how it is done right!"

Ammaji took her sweet time to refold all the clothes. "Watch me," Ammaji said, and laid the last piece of clothing, an underwear, on the floor. She stretched it, taking out the wrinkles, then folded it in three and then over once more. "See?" she said.

Gauri wanted to ask why she spent so much time on each piece of clothing when they would be tossed into the laundry chute again tomorrow. But out of respect, she kept her mouth shut. "Here, done the right way!" Ammaji said, and pushed the basket of refolded clothes toward Gauri. "Now you can take these upstairs!" Gauri knew the routine. She picked up the basket and turned to walk upstairs. At that moment she noticed the front door was slightly ajar. She placed the basket on the first step and opened the door wide. A view of the weeping willow's swaying branches came into view. Like a welcome companion, a soft wind brought in the sweet smell of the late spring day.

"Close that door, *Bahu*!" Ammaji grumbled from the kitchen.

Gauri jumped and shut the door to the world. Hurriedly, she picked up the basket and strode upstairs to distribute the folded clothes to their respective bedrooms and their allotted spaces.

Since her first day, Ramji had been leaving early and returning either after evening tea or just before dinner was served. During the summer months, he traveled extensively. Almost every week, he flew to one state or another. But on the days he was home, the family atmosphere was cheerful. While Boji could be affectionate, most of the time he was indifferent. Ammaji, it seemed to Gauri, wore her position of power as mother like armor, closing her heart and mind to the changed circumstances of the family. The only person Gauri could communicate with was her husband, and she began feeling genuine love for the man she had married.

On one such day, they all gathered around the kitchen table. Ammaji served a plate of steamed rice, lamb, spinach, and lotus root first to Boji and then to Ramji. Gauri poured them glasses of plain buttermilk. When Ramji asked Gauri to eat with him, she politely refused. How did he expect her to eat while Ammaji was still serving? When the two women started their dinner, Boji returned to his reading and Ramji made business calls.

Dinner was over and leftovers stored in Tupperware containers. The table was wiped clean, and pots, pans, dishes, and silverware hand washed and dried (although they had a dishwasher). The floor was swept. By now, Gauri had become used to Ammaji redoing the things she did. The redoing made her mundane chores even less appealing. But these were the ways of the Raina family. Her mother had told her they would be different, and she would have to learn to adjust to them. The only time Ammaji did not or could not redo what she had done was the time Gauri spent with Ramji.

#

One day after lunch, Gauri settled on a chair near the bay window in her room that looked over the weeping willow in the front yard. A letter to her parents was overdue. In the first month of her marriage, she had written weekly, but now it was once or twice a month. She wrote slowly, *My dearest Maji and Molaji*, but before she could continue, her hand seemed to take over: It drew the willow tree and the trees and plants now laden with summer flowers. It drew the row of houses on the other side of the street. When Gauri first began, she was using a blue ballpoint, but by the time the drawing was finished, she had added color with red and black ballpoints. That was all she had.

One after the other, she turned the pages of the letter pad and sketched several versions of the scene. Then she remembered the cityscape view from the bathroom window with its fluttering flag and early spring sun. She walked to the bathroom and sketched that scene from the window. As the sketch emerged on the pad, a pleasant feeling she had not felt in months enveloped her. She would paint in oil when she had art materials. Each time she mentioned buying brushes, paints, and canvas to Ramji, he changed the subject. She wondered why.

"Gauri! Come downstairs. It's almost teatime." Ammaji's voice stilled her thoughts and brought her back to the present.

"Coming!" she shouted.

The summer months dragged by. Ramji still had not found time to drive Gauri to the store to buy art materials. Recently, Ramji had traveled to Philadelphia, New York, and D.C. to check out his franchises that sold Kashmiri shawls, silk saris, papier-mâché boxes and bowls, walnut carvings for walls, and sculptural decorative pieces. The business was thriving because of his personal attention and the guidance of his new partner, Mr. Sen. He was planning to add a new store in the Boston area. When he was home, a large chunk of his time was spent at his Pittsburgh store, the rest with his parents, and nights intertwining his body with Gauri's. It was pleasurable for both, but Gauri craved friendship. She wanted someone she could talk to about the finer things in life, about painting, about the difference between art and banality, about nature and the new landscapes in her new country. Several times when Ramji and she sat together, she tried to start such a conversation with him, but his mind was more on business than on art, crafts, and aesthetics. Did he not remember that she was an artist? Did he not recall the day they first met and he admired her paintings?

One fall evening, after Ramji and Boji had finished eating and Ammaji and Gauri were quietly having dinner, the ringing telephone broke the silence. "That must be Sukumar!" Ramji said, grabbing the phone as he sat at the kitchen table. Boji bid them good night and left. Dinner was over and the kitchen cleaned. Ramji was still on the phone. Ammaji went upstairs to her room, leaving the young couple alone. As soon as Ramji hung up the phone, Gauri looked straight into Ramji's eyes and said, "Is your work ever done?"

"I am sitting here next to you, am I not?"

"Not really! You were sitting with Sukumar or—"

"You look at everything from your angle, always criticizing!" Ramji frowned.

"Who else's angle am I going to look from? Criticizing? I haven't begun yet! I've been waiting for a moment like this for months," Gauri said and stood up.

"What about last Sunday?" Ramji frowned.

"What about it?"

"We went for dinner."

"You said you would take me out so that we could talk," she said, pointing her finger first at him and then at herself. "But we didn't!"

"And before dinner, I took you to a movie! It wasn't cheap," he said, pressing his index finger to the tip of her nose.

"That's not funny! Going to the movies is not conversing, not having a heart-to-heart talk!" His saying "it wasn't cheap" echoed in her mind.

"No, it is not! What is there to talk about? We had fun. We watched a movie, we ate out."

"You promised we'd go to the art store."

"Ammaji and Boji were tired. They wanted to come home."

"Why couldn't we go to the art store first, as I had asked?"

"What do they have to do with the art store?"

"What does that even mean? I needed to buy art supplies. You treat me like I'm of no significance to you, just the help."

"How dare you?"

"You may not see anything wrong with our relationship, but I do. I won't be silenced!" Gauri got up and left.

"What the hell!" Ramji muttered to himself.

Later in bed, he profusely apologized. They made up, and Gauri hoped for better days ahead.

On a Sunday afternoon, during the family siesta hour, Gauri settled at her usual place next to the bay window and sketched on her pad with colored ball-point pens.

"Here you are!" It was Ramji standing at the door. "Why don't you sit downstairs with us?"

She turned to look at him. Pointing to the other chair in front of the window she said, "Come sit with me for a while!"

"No, come downstairs. What will they think?" He did not move.

"Think about what?" she said, raising her eye-brows.

"I hardly spend any time with them! They're old, you know. Come downstairs."

"I want to finish this sketch. I'll come when I'm done," she said and continued to draw. She heard him leave in a huff.

What was wrong with this family? Ammaji was obsessed with cleaning, Boji consumed by daily papers, and Ramji over-occupied with his business. And when her husband was home, he was feeling guilty for not spending enough time with his aging parents. She never had a chunk of time with her husband, and when not assisting the family matriarch, she was left to herself. She thought the family routine before and after Ramji's marriage was unchanged.

The winter months felt like years. The routine of house cleaning did not change with the changing weather. Outside, the trees were barren. Rust, gold, and brown leaves buried beneath the white. Inside, though, the two women continued to dust and mop and polish floors and furniture and china. The cleaner the house got, the darker Gauri's world felt.

Gauri's imagination and creative flow was slowly turning as frigid as the winter. The daily paper and television was filled with news about unfamiliar people, events, and things. Those things that she had thought were fundamental to her existence became insignificant, and the things she thought unimportant were forced upon her daily routine. Her world was topsy-turvy, and she felt powerless to change it. On rare occasions when she tried to doodle, her hand hesitated and the lines wavered. It was as if she was playing notes but could hear no music.

One day, when the lunch dishes were done and Boji had left to take his afternoon nap, Gauri asked, "Ammaji, may I say something? Ammaji, poking at her teeth with a toothpick, had been walking up the steps, and Gauri was standing at the landing.

"Go ahead," she said with furrowed brows.

Gripping the banister and clearing her throat, Gauri said, "Why don't we clean the house every other day?" It had been an effort to say those words aloud.

"Why not take your bath every other day?" she snapped. "But why do you ask?"

Gauri flinched. "I need a few mornings a week to do my own work."

"What work?" Ammaji stood still, her left foot on a lower step and her right on the one she was about to climb.

"Artwork! Painting!" She wanted to throw her hands in the air but controlled herself. "I must make time to paint."

"You can do that after lunch." Ammaji climbed a couple more steps.

"But I am tired by then. I do my best work in the morning." She spoke unhesitatingly.

"What is there to painting strokes and making pencil lines? One can do it any time of the day."

"No, I can't!"

"If we wanted a busy daughter-in-law, my son would have married a girl who was doing a regular job, earning money. We received so many proposals—*Bahut rishte aye*, the matchmaker brought so many girls to our attention. A doctor, professor, engineer—the girls were highly recommended. I don't know what he saw . . ."

Ammaji walked up the rest of the steps but stopped in the hallway and looked down at Gauri. She said, "How much money can you earn as a painter? See that painting in the living room? I brought it on sale for twenty-five dollars!"

"It's not about money; that's not why I do it," Gauri mumbled to herself. She remembered cringing at the sight of that painting the moment she had set eyes on it.

"Then what is it about?"

"It is food for my soul—the only thing that nourishes me, makes me feel good and free."

"You're starting to talk like American women. What is this free-shree? You are a married woman now. Forget art-shart, forget free-shree!"

"There are married painters in the world, good ones, and some unmarried ones as well."

"Not in this house! Make art? What for?" Ammaji walked away and disappeared into her bedroom.

Standing in the hallway between the living room and dining room, Gauri gazed at the things surrounding her: the walnut wood furniture, love seat, maharaja chair, brass bowl on the center table, soft cushions, silk carpet, papier-mâché plates, walnut swans hanging on the walls, and the ugly painting in the living room. And then she walked upstairs past the two guest bedrooms facing Ammaji and Boji's room, and into her room.

She felt the gray shaggy carpet with her feet and looked up at the smooth ceiling, then at the neatly made bed, the window, and the drapes. The towels in her bathroom were folded, hanging on the racks. So were the hand towels that matched the mats on the floor and soaps on the sink. Even the talcum powder and aftershave echoed the same color. The soap, powder, and lotion would still be there when she was gone, gone forever. When she was gone, what of her would be left behind? What would be her legacy? Clean rooms? Folded laundry?

To clear her mind, she took a walk. Pulling on a warm jacket and cap, she wrapped a scarf around her neck and put on her gloves. It was a sunny afternoon. Under the milky-blue sky, silver dollar bushes were in full bloom. She crossed the lawn, turned left onto the road, and walked along the neighborhood sidewalks cleared of snow, until her legs began to ache and her nose and lips felt numb. When she turned back, an image of a bouquet of silver dollar branches arranged in a vase appeared in her mind. From the front of the house, she collected a few branches and brought them inside. Lest she drop any debris on the floor, she carefully took them to the kitchen sink, trimmed the extra leaves and stem ends, and arranged them in a blue-black ceramic vase with gold specks—one of the vases she had saved from flowers sent by Ramji's business acquaintances.

Removing her jacket, she put the arrangement on the dining table and went to fetch her sketchpad and ballpoint pens from her bedroom. When she returned, the flowers had disappeared! Where did they go?

"There were bugs in those flowers, Gauri!" Ammaji called from somewhere in the house. "They would have spread everywhere. Why did you bring them into the house?"

"I checked, Ammaji. There are no bugs in this frigid weather!" Gauri called back. "There aren't any bugs. The branches look beautiful in the sunlight. I want to draw them. Where did you put them?"

"I threw them in the garbage. It's time for you to take a nap!" she shouted back.

Gauri looked in the trash. The silvery bouquet glowed even in the dump! Ammaji had put the vase back with other ones. She ran to her room and sobbed bitterly.

Gauri had to think hard, really hard. She was once again going to have a heart-to-heart talk with Ramji. After dinner that night, she waited for him to come to the bedroom.

He finally came, changed into his nightclothes, brushed his teeth, and brought a file to bed. Before he could open it, though, she turned to him and said, "Ramji, do you think I can use part of the basement as my studio?"

"Hmmm," Ramji mumbled. "What did you say?"

"Would it be okay if I use part of the basement to paint?"

"No, not the basement! Don't you know that's Ammaji's pantry and storage?"

"Pantry, yes, but in the rest of the space is stored what seems to be junk—discarded appliances, broken furniture, old electronic gadgets. Why can't we get rid of that stuff?"

"Don't say that in front of her! You would hurt her feelings. Boji and I once accused her of being a hoarder, and all hell broke loose!"

"I don't want to hurt her feelings. I simply need a space to paint; otherwise I'll go crazy. I can find the time, but without a designated space, I can't work."

"This wouldn't be such a problem if you simply wouldn't think about painting!"

"You don't know what you are doing to me! If I don't paint, I'll suffocate. Painting is my life; to become an artist is my dream. I must paint the way a koel bird must sing."

Ramji closed his file with a snap. "I didn't know I had married a philosopher! Do whatever you want to do, but don't disturb Ammaji's space." With his file under his arm, he got up and left the room.

"Where are you going?"

"To work in the kitchen!"

Gauri had thought if she talked to Ramji about how she felt, he might do something or say something that would salve her emotional wounds; instead, he had sprinkled chili pepper on them. She didn't ask him to stay.

Early the next morning, Ramji drove Ammaji and Boji to the home of a family friend for a day of *satsang*, a devotional gathering. That evening, he was to drive them back home. They asked Gauri to accompany them, but she said she was not feeling well.

Gauri's sketchpad was almost filled. She had used almost all the ballpoint pens that she could get her hands on. The last time Ramji returned from a business conference, he had emptied his briefcase and given Gauri a bunch of pens with the names and logos of different companies. All sorts of new compositions and visions emerged from her imagination. But the scene that she had been struck by the first day she arrived in Pittsburgh always remained at the back of her mind.

She sketched various versions of the view from the bathroom window. With blue, black, and red pens, she made a line sketch, then used the chiaroscuro technique to solidify forms. She squinted and examined her work, drew some more, squinted and looked again. She drew the brick houses and American flags brilliant in red, white, and blue. She filled the blue sky with floating white clouds, then drew the horizon and fresh grass at the bottom of the page. The scene slowly emerged, and she looked at it with some satisfaction. She realized the final composition did not meet her approval, but at least she had made visible what so far had been real only in her imagination. Her cheeks were flushed from hours of concentration and the release of pent-up emotions. Yes, she was going to paint it on a large canvas in oils. This would be her first painting in America.

"Gauri! Gauri, please come down! Would you make us some tea?" Ramji's voice startled her. She had lost track of time and had not heard them return. She closed her sketchbook.

"What have you been doing?" Ramji was standing behind her.

"You scared me!" she said, turning around. "You are back earlier than I had expected."

"What? Doodling again?" He smirked and picked up one of the many sketches she had drawn that afternoon.

"Yes, you may call them doodles." Gauri gathered the scattered sketches and put them on the sketchbook. "Ramji, I must talk to you," she said

"About what?"

"I must work, otherwise I'll go mad. Do you think I can find some work?"

"Outside the home?"

"Yes, something to do with art."

"Why not at home? Why outside?"

"You know why. Besides, if I earn money, I wouldn't need to ask you for it. Buying art materials seems to be waste of money for you. So many times I asked you to buy me some, but you didn't."

"I got your paintings framed, didn't I? What else do you want me to do?"

"Drive me to an art store or just give me money so I can get a taxi and buy the supplies I need."

"Why spend so much on a stupid hobby?"

"I have told you so many times, Ramji, it is not my hobby, it's my life."

"There you go again philosophizing—'my life.'" He turned to leave and mumbled, "And by the way, you can't work outside the home."

"Wait!" Gauri said to his back. "Did you say I can't work outside the home?"

"Yes, something like that!" Ramji stopped.

"Why not?" Gauri asked.

"No woman from this house has or will ever work outside the home. And you are not going to break that tradition! Besides, why would a woman want to work like a lower caste? Especially when I earn enough?"

"What has work to do with caste or gender?"

"Your thinking is screwed up. I want no more discussion of your stupid art!" Ramji left, slamming the door behind him.

Gauri got up from the chair and climbed onto the bed. She sat with her arms wrapped around her legs and rocked herself. Everything was strange, foreign. Nothing belonged to her. Nothing had any meaning. How could her parents have agreed to this match? Why did she?

A shiver raced up her spine. She pulled up the blanket lying on the bed and wrapped it around herself. It did not warm her. The cold was inside her. She pulled the blanket a little tighter and mourned her skill, dying from lack of practice, the skill she had worked so hard to acquire. Her budding talent was withering before it had had an opportunity to blossom. What her parents thought to be a well-established, modern household was an outdated, outmoded conservative hell. The man she had mistaken to be a connoisseur of the arts turned out to be a philistine. What had been her hurry to get married? Why had she not insisted on delaying the marriage? The day the matchmaker had brought the marriage proposal to her parents, the curator had given her the dates when the Lake Palace Art Gallery—one of the major galleries—was available for her second show. At that crossroad, she had taken the wrong turn. How was she going to mend that mistake?

What was she to do now? Have a few children? Ammaji wanted grandchildren, preferably grandsons. Her aunt had advised her not to have a baby right away. "Get settled first," she had said. "Go to your doctor and get an IUD." Gauri had followed her advice before the wedding day.

Was Ramji a good husband? Would he be a good father? Would they ever move to a home of their own? Ammaji was stern, meddling, and a clean freak, but she was not a villain. Perhaps it was Gauri's own fault for not trying harder to "get adjusted" to her new life.

Another spring arrived. The house Gauri thought would be her haven was like a detention center. She was trundling on a treadmill without any hope of reaching a destination. Then she met someone who had been within her reach for some time, though she had no way of knowing.

Gauri had heard Ramji talk about Sukumar Sen so often, but she had not given him a second thought. Then Ramji and Gauri were invited to his home for dinner, and she was curious to meet him and his wife. While driving to the Sens' home, she learned that he was in his mid-sixties, a decade older than his wife. They had two grown children, a son and a daughter who lived in the city in their own apartments. She had often heard Ammaji talk disapprovingly about that arrangement. "Is that how a good Indian family lives? Parents in one house, son in another, and daughter in the third one, alone! Only in Amreekah could they do this!"

Ramji parked his Lexus in front of the Sens' house: a cottage nestled in maples and oaks with blossoming mauve philodendron and yellow azalea bushes in front. Mrs. Sen, dressed in a chocolate-colored silk sari with a yellow and gold border, greeted the two with a smile, giving Gauri a gentle hug. She led them through a foyer lit by the orange light of the setting sun. A miniature waterfall, with green and yellow foliage framing a statue of the Buddha seated in meditation, welcomed them. She led them to a spacious drawing room and asked them to sit. Gauri and Ramji sat on a sofa with soft camel-colored cushions and rested her arm on a mahogany armrest. The sofa and other chairs' feet were carved into lions' claws. The coffee and side tables were of the same wood. In one corner, a spotlight showcased a bronze statue of Nataraj, the lord of the dance. On the floor beside the mantelpiece were stacks of art books, the one on top open. The warmth of this place was palpable. The mantelpiece, laden with framed photographs, attracted Gauri's attention.

"Your children?" Gauri asked.

"Yes," Mrs. Sen said, "our daughter and our son. She is a psychologist, and he teaches math at the Sewickley High School. They live here in Pittsburgh . . ."

Just then, Mr. Sen walked in carrying a tray with four glasses and a jug of lemonade. "Hi, folks! Enough about our children, Kappu! She is very proud of them!" he said to Gauri. Gauri nodded in agreement, and Sen's wife, Kapila, excused herself.

"Deservingly so," Ramji said. "Shouldn't she be?"

"Of course, of course! But not at the expense of neglecting the guests," Mr. Sen said good-naturedly, pouring drinks and handing them to Ramji and Gauri.

Mrs. Sen returned with plates of hot samosas and pakoras and tamarind and mint chutneys. She served the snacks, patting each guest's shoulder as she passed.

What poise, what warmth, Gauri thought of Mrs. Sen. Her likable personality resonated with her, and she found her hard to resist.

A bite of the samosa stirred Gauri's taste buds. "Delicious!" she said. "You're a good cook."

"Store bought, Deep Frozen Foods, I only fried them. Thanks anyway," Mrs. Sen said.

"I must remember that name," Gauri said. "Deep Frozen Foods. I'm still getting used to this country."

A timer in the kitchen beeped. Kapila placed her plate on the table and said, "If you want, you can come to the kitchen with me." Gauri eagerly followed.

"Double adjustment in your case—a new family, a foreign country," Kapila said as she turned the timer off.

"What?"

"I said in your case you have to make two adjustments."

"Oh yes! But you know it won't bother me so much if I could. . .when I get back to work."

"How long has it been? A year?"

"One year, two weeks, and one day," Gauri said.

"Long year, hmm?"

"Sometimes it feels very, verrrry long." Gauri was surprised at her openness. The older woman nodded with a sympathetic smile. Gauri wanted to tell her more about how she felt, but she had just met her.

"Let me show you around the house," Mrs. Sen said. While their husbands discussed business, she took Gauri for a tour of her home. They walked through the family room, a sunroom, and a few hallways. Indian and American paintings in different styles hung on white walls. Bamboo stands held green philodendron and purple orchids in brass pots, which stood against the walls between the paintings. The floor in each room was covered with a carpet or a dhurrie rug.

"Your home is so beautiful, Mrs. Sen! Who cleans it?"

"You can call me Kapila. A lady comes to clean it."

"Every day?"

"Oh no, no! Twice a month."

In one corner of the kitchen counter, Gauri noticed a collection of hand-carved mortar and pestle sets from different regions of India. A pottery bowl held fresh herbs, and a vase held kitchen utensils. Everything seemed to have been placed playfully yet artistically throughout the house, reflecting the personality of the couple.

"I love how you have decorated your house," Gauri said.

Mrs. Sen said, "Thank you!"

One could not create a home like this overnight. It needed a lifetime of authentic living to emanate such a rich and artistic ambiance. Their life, like their home, seemed like a work of art. Gauri tried to imagine her own home feeling like this.

"Your taste is impeccable!" Gauri said before they rejoined Ramji and Mr. Sen, who by now had moved to the family room.

Mrs. Sen sat next to Gauri and said, "By the way, Gauri, a person who appreciates art like that must have a strong sense of aesthetics; tell me, are you an artist?"

"I thought you knew! Yes, I am an artist." Gauri covered her mouth in embarrassment.

"Don't be embarrassed! Now why didn't Ramji mention it? Which art school did you go to?"

"Shantiniketan."

"Shantiniketan! That school is a phenomenon. Many years ago, I was there on a one-semester sabbatical. Which medium?"

"Oil painting."

The look on Mrs. Sen's face changed. For a moment, she seemed to be lost in thought. She asked, "Do you paint now? Or maybe I should ask when do you plan to start painting again?"

"I don't have the time or a place to paint," Gauri whispered.

"Hmm . . .," Mrs. Sen said. Then she turned to Ramji, who was busy talking to Mr. Sen on the other side of the room. "Hey, mister, you are lucky to be married to an artist."

"Am I lucky or she is?" Ramji said sheepishly. From her husband's awkward smile, Gauri sensed that he felt intimidated by Kapila.

Ignoring his comment, Kapila said, "Don't let her talent go to waste. Graduated from Shantiniketan! They graduate the cream of the crop, you know." Ramji either didn't understand or pretended not to, for he said nothing.

After their visit to the Sens, the two drove home in silence. Mrs. Sen had inspired Gauri and stirred in her a desire she had been trying to suppress for more than a year. There had been a constant battle between the Gauri who led a listless life against her will and wants, and the Gauri who desired to be an artist. Mrs. Sen had made her aware that her life as an artist had been slipping away during that year. Her years at the art school and then at home were a mere waste of time and talent if she did not act on that deep driving desire.

A few days after the fateful meeting with Mrs. Sen, Gauri and Ramji were driving home from his favorite butcher shop. He was in a good mood, singing along to a tune on the radio, his hand tapping the steering wheel. She gathered the courage to again ask him for his permission to work. As the Raina family no longer lived in India but in a country where individual freedom was fundamental, was it possible for them to bend their family "tradition"? Maybe make the pioneering move of allowing a woman work outside the home?

When Gauri asked the question, Ramji became serious. He stopped humming, switched off the radio, and gripped the steering wheel. He did not turn his head but looked straight ahead at the road. For a few miles, they drove in silence.

Gauri waited for him to say something, but he didn't, so she asked, "Ramji, did you hear me?"

With his left hand on the steering wheel and his right on Gauri's thigh, Ramji said, "I don't understand, Gauri. Why do you want to work? Aren't you happy?" He gently squeezed her.

"Would you be happy if you couldn't do the one thing that made you happy?"

"Don't I love you? Aren't you comfortable? Why isn't that enough? Besides, it is different with women. See how happy my mother is?"

Gauri pushed his hand away. He rubbed his neck then put his hand on the wheel.

"Is she?" Gauri said as she thought of Ammaji. "I have never seen her smile. Laughter is out of question. But when we are cleaning the house she hums, at times even sings. The rest of the time, she looks annoyed."

He ignored her remarks. "If you work, who will help my mother with cleaning and cooking?"

"First of all, we don't have to clean the house every day. Second, we can hire a cleaning agency. Ammaji is growing older. She can't continue to do the cleaning and washing and cooking by herself."

"That she won't allow. She won't let an agency clean her house. Besides, there are other things to be done."

"I'll help her cook when I come home," Gauri said.

"She won't like it."

Gauri shrank in her seat. Her muscles tightened and her teeth clenched. "I don't know how to make you understand why I must paint."

"Why?"

"Because I must . . .because it is my lifeline . . . because since I was ten years old—" Gauri pleaded. "I don't know how to explain, how to make you understand that without art, my life is meaningless. It connects me to something greater than myself and makes me feel alive, and afterward, a rich feeling lingers deep within my soul."

He turned his head, looked at her in awe, then turned back to look through the windshield and said, "You are losing it." He did not wait for her to say anything before he continued, "Same thing over and over again, same thing! You sound like a parrot: work, work, work! You don't need to work; I have told you a hundred times that it is beneath us to work. I earn enough for both of us!" He sucked his teeth, which he did when he was enraged and out of control.

They did not talk for the rest of the day. That night in bed, Ramji started to snore as soon as his head hit the pillow. Gauri tossed and turned.

She had lost the self-assurance she had possessed when she first stepped into Ramji's house. So far, her longing for self-expression had been stifled. She had closed her self to it. The small sparks of creativity within begged her to follow a different path, one where she was free to pour her passion and emotions into colors and forms. Did he ever think of redrawing his life's map? She had been forced to redraw hers after marrying him.

The following month, when Ramji informed the family that he had invited the Sens for dinner, Gauri couldn't wait. She heard Ammaji say to him, "I don't see why you associate with those people. They have forgotten their Hindu traditions; they have lost their path. Their children live in separate homes—rotten Amreekan culture!"

"Can't control their own children! They themselves behave like pseudo-Amreekans, especially the wife," added Boji.

"But their children are adults, and they are Americans!" Ramji said, although he rarely contradicted his parents. This gave Gauri a sliver of hope. He looked at her and gave a wink.

"That will never happen in this house." Ammaji and Boji were together on this.

But on the evening of the dinner, Ammaji was everywhere: in the kitchen ladling, at the sink rinsing, near the counter wiping, at the dinner table serving, while Gauri assisted. The two of them joined the guests only after everyone had second servings. Boji ate with relish and gestured for more. Throughout the dinner, Ramji and Mr. Sen discussed how they could increase the sale prices of their merchandize without jeopardizing their business. Mrs. Sen talked courteously with Ammaji and asked Gauri if she had made any paintings. Gauri shook her head.

After dinner, Ammaji and Boji excused themselves. Bidding everyone good night, they retired to their room.

Gauri went to the kitchen to make tea and overheard Mrs. Sen say, "Hey, Ramji, what about helping your bride?"

"She is not a bride anymore! Does she need my help?" Ramji said.

Gauri returned with a tray of teacups filled with masala tea and a plate of pistachio burfi. She saw Ramji smiling sheepishly at Mrs. Sen. As she was about to set the tray on the table, Ramji said, "Let's have tea in the family room." So she carried the tray to the room where her husband wanted to sit.

"Can I help with anything?" Mrs. Sen picked up a few remaining water goblets and plates from the dining table and followed Gauri.

"No, please, Mrs. Sen, I want you to sit."

"Kapila, please, and that's all right; I don't mind," Mrs. Sen said as she placed the plates in the sink. "So show me some of your art. Have you been painting?"

Gauri shrugged. "I don't seem to have the time or inspiration to do as much as I would like." She offered her guest a piece of the sweet pistachio burfi. "I don't even have supplies to work with. The practice of my art has hit a brick wall. Honestly, Kapila, why would the muses stick around? They seem to have left me."

"Muses never leave, dear. Without practice, they just go dormant." Mrs. Sen declined the dessert with a gentle sweep of her hand. "Show me something you've painted."

Gauri hesitated, looking toward the doorway to the family room. "Okay," she said.

She led Kapila to her bedroom. The three watercolors that she had persuaded Ramji to frame hung on the wall opposite the window. Mrs. Sen stood at a distance and looked at each one. "These are beautiful! Tell me about them."

"This one is called Morning at the Yarbal," replied Gauri, pointing to the one depicting a riverbank. "I painted this scene from my father's study, which overlooks the riverfront." Touching the frame in the middle, Gauri said, "This is Woman in a Houseboat Cooking Rice." Gauri remembered sketching the scene while on a boat ride with Molaji and Maji. She had sketched the houseboat on which a family lived, as the boat she was in glided by. Quickly, she had drawn the woman ladling water from the river into the rice pot that was on a clay stove.

Gauri told Mrs. Sen that on their way home, after she had made numerous sketches, the sketchbook had fallen into the river and sunk. Seeing her distress, her parents had coaxed her to paint the scene from memory. She had imagined the composition and painted the picture at home.

Gauri pointed at the third painting, Sunset at the Wedding. The memory of that evening flashed through Gauri's mind. Seated on a tonga with her parents, she had heard the clip-clop of hooves as the horses galloped through the walnut and apple orchards. Fields of tender rice plants edged with daffodils spread out for miles. Daub-and-wattle homes were silhouetted against the distant blue sky. When the tonga stopped, the chorus of wedding songs chimed in her ears.

"Are these the only paintings you brought with you?" Mrs. Sen asked.

"No, I have more."

Gauri gathered a pile of large drawings and a small bundle of sketches that she had unwrapped when she arrived. One by one, she spread the drawings on the bed and floor. Mrs. Sen closely examined the ones on the bed and squatted on the floor, looking with great interest at the drawings. When she stood, she placed her hand on Gauri's shoulder and said, "I'm no expert, but I can tell that's good work. I need to put you in touch with my friend who owns an art gallery. You must not give up. You have to continue this somehow."

Gauri did not say a word. She gathered the drawings into a pile and put them back in the credenza drawer. When she turned, Mrs. Sen was gazing at the watercolors on the wall. Her genuine interest in the paintings emboldened Gauri.

"Mrs. Sen, people keep telling me to come down to earth," Gauri said. "Why should I if the sky is better? They say, 'Wake up, Gauri, don't daydream!' Why shouldn't I? When my eyes are closed, I see images. But I deny them, block them, bury them, muffle them. I am an artist but cannot paint. I keep telling people I'm an artist. I'm invisible to them because they do not see my work's worth. They say, 'You have everything; why aren't you happy, why aren't you satisfied with what you have? Once you have little ones, will you be painting?' They think if I have children, I'm going to grow into something different. They don't understand I want to paint until I die. They insist it's just a hobby. Can art ever be just a hobby? What a nonsensical idea, Kapila! I will never, never put my feet on the muddy ground. I will gaze above and scream, 'If you don't understand art, you do not have a soul . . . you do not have a soul.'" As Gauri said this, she burst into sobs.

Mrs. Sen put her arm around Gauri, hugged her tightly, and sat next to her on the bed as she cried.

"I'm so sorry Mrs. Sen . . . so, so sorry. I didn't mean to blurt that out." Gauri wiped her eyes, blew her nose with a handkerchief, and looked at Mrs. Sen as if she were a sister, a mother, and a mentor to her.

"I'm glad you've lightened your heart. A good cry clears the mind of fog. And listen, Gauri, a good friend, a business partner of mine, Henry Drummond, has a gallery. He is looking for someone to take the place of Fernando."

"Who is Fernando?"

"Henry's art apprentice."

"Why is he leaving?"

"He worked there for two years and wants to go home to Mexico. He lives in a one-room apartment behind the gallery, works part-time and paints in a small studio in his apartment. Would you like to work there? You don't have to live there."

"What would I do?"

"Help with sales, show artwork to customers, and take care of the general upkeep of the place."

Gauri lowered her eyes. "What would my family say? They won't like it. They will say, 'What, work as a salesperson!'"

"Freedom doesn't come free, Gauri; you need to be courageous, fight for your rights! Millions of beautiful dreams will continue to be crushed until women like you gather courage to rebel and change the status quo. You cannot elevate the quality of your life unless you are determined. You cannot actualize your potential without courage. You need to believe that the universe will come to your rescue if you are fearless. Gauri, you cannot remain passive. You must fight for your rights and freedom. This pattern will not break unless you act boldly," Mrs. Sen said.

When she met Gauri's gaze, she added, "Think about it! The job is yours if you want it."

Gauri couldn't wait for the evening to be over so she could tell Ramji about Mrs. Sen's proposal, but he was tired and went straight to bed when the guests left.

Gauri kept thinking about the conversation she had with Mrs. Sen as she cleaned up. She was glad she had this time to soften her feelings and allow her excitement to subside before blurting out her emotions and thoughts to Ramji. But when she got up the next morning, Ramji had already left.

Later that evening when Ramji returned home, he sat on the family room sofa reading the daily paper. Ammaji was in the kitchen and Boji in his room. Gauri sat next to him and told him about Kapila's job offer.

"What? Listen to yourself!" He sat up. "Has it come down to this—a Raina woman working as a saleswoman? I don't want you to utter a word about this crazy idea to Ammaji or Boji—you would be insulting them. A saleswoman!"

"Sorry!" she said, "Don't scream!"

Tears flowed down her face as she ran upstairs to her bedroom and closed the door. Breathing heavily, she paced from the wall to the window. Anger clouded her thinking. What should she do? Baffled, her heart raced, and she sat at the edge of her bed. Suddenly, she walked to the vanity, took out the bundle of ballpoint sketches she had made, held them tightly under her arm and ran down the steps to the kitchen. She heard Ramji arguing in low tones with his parents in the family room. She yanked open the kitchen drawer that contained the neatly piled stack of matchboxes. The drawer flew off the tracks and crashed to the floor. Forks and spoons, colored rubber bands, coupons tied in a bundle, and a box of toothpicks scattered onto the floor. She gritted her teeth, looked at the mess, and picked up a matchbox.

She opened the door to the backyard and slammed it as she walked out. Standing in the middle of the yard, she struck a match and lit the sketches. The flames rose as the paper burned and turned to ashes. Ramji came out outside and ran towards her, but her gaze was focused on the burning edges of the sketches.

"Are you mad?" he screamed as he snatched the bundle from her grip. Throwing it on the grass, he stomped on the bundle with his leather sandals. When the fire was out, he led her back to their bedroom. "Tsk, tsk." He shook his head. "You should see a psychiatrist," he said, slamming the door behind him as he left. Gauri felt like punching his face, but she resisted the urge to run after him. She had a throbbing headache, and her mind was foggy. How could she have set fire to her own art? Her eyes welled with liquid anger.

And then suddenly a calm came all over Gauri. She picked up the phone and called Kapila.

Ramji did not come to bed that night.

At midnight, Gauri went to the kitchen to get a drink. The light was on, and she overheard Ammaji and Ramji talking.

"That was very foolish of you to quarrel with your wife outside your home. What will the neighbors say?" Ammaji said.

"A drama. That was a drama she enacted. Stupid, stupid art! Sacrifice, she says! What is she sacrificing if she can't devote her life to the family?" Ramji said through clenched teeth.

"Women must sacrifice! I sacrificed my whole life for the sake of this family! What did I get in return? But do I complain?"

"Amma, no matter what I tell you, you blabber about your own life story: 'Oh, how exceptionally talented I was, and I sacrificed all of that for the sake of this family!' I have heard this a thousand times. Would you shut up and listen to me for once?" Ramji yelled.

"No, I'm not going to shut up! You listen to me! I won awards in singing, but once I married, I knew my responsibility: A woman's dharma is to sacrifice everything for the sake of her family's welfare. For a woman, family comes first; what has she to do with a career? The two are as different as water and oil. Your wife should have been born a man. It is not difficult to understand! Why can't you make your wife understand this?"

"She is stubborn. She won't listen, and she's always complaining."

"Did I complain when your father refused to hire a tabla accompanist for me to practice? Didn't I dedicate my whole life to you and your father? By the time you were born, I did not even remember that I used to sing. Didn't I help you choose a wife who would not work outside the home?" Ammaji's voice trembled.

"Yes, yes, and yes, Amma. Now stop!"

Then there was quiet.

Stunned, Gauri tiptoed back to her room.

Ramji left for work very early that morning. Gauri unhooked the three watercolors from the wall of her bedroom and tied them together. She pulled the stack of larger drawings from the credenza and rolled them up. She placed them in a suitcase over some clothes on which she had pressed down her drawing book. Closing the suitcase, she also zipped up the duffel bag with things she had brought to America.

Gauri heard Ammaji pushing the furniture against the walls. She dialed the number for a cab. Removing the red envelope she had taped to her drawing book, she took the cash and placed it in her purse. Carrying her luggage down the steps and out to the curb, she waited for the cab to arrive.

"Gauri!" She saw Ammaji walking down the front steps. "Where are you going with all this luggage?" Ammaji's eyebrows narrowed, and her lips parted in shock.

"I need to go somewhere, to think and decide whether my life is to be lived for my husband or for my art."

"How will you live? What will you eat? Come back. What will people say? Ramji is your provider; you can't leave him!" Ammaji said, her hands shaking.

"I can't live here any longer," Gauri said.

When their gazes met, Ammaji had a blank expression on her face. *Was that anger or a glimmer of hope?* She wondered. When she looked again, Ammaji's face had become stern. She turned her back to Gauri and stiffly walked back inside.

The cab arrived, and the driver nodded to Gauri as he picked up the luggage. She got into the cab and heard the trunk slam. A small American flag was hanging from the rearview mirror. The cabbie slid into the driver's seat and watched her gazing at the flag. He had a smile on his face.

"Where to, ma'am?" His voice was thick with an unfamiliar accent.

"To the Drummond Art Gallery on Craig Street," Gauri replied.

She looked back at the house. She felt detached from it, and for the first time, she could feel her fear turn to courage and her outrage to compassion.

THE BLACKENED MIRROR

I was a portrait painter. Young and self-taught. I started by copying black-and-white images of wrinkled old people, famished children, laborers carrying loads, and farmers plowing fields: all laboring for food and shelter. I knew their pain, their suffering. My mother was a bricklayer, and I, a dreamer. Each of us owned two sets of clothing: one covered our body and the other hung daily in the sun to dry. My mother worked hard for the builder to provide us with two meals a day, but I was content with only one if I could buy art supplies to depict moments in people's lives.

From the time I was nine until I turned sixteen, my aim was to feel at one with the person I painted. I also became conscious of my mother's struggle to survive. I sold my first work for a pittance. My mother tried persuading me to be a bricklayer, but she did not succeed. The day she discovered what I did while she was at the construction site, she hit me hard, so hard that I bled. From then on, I hid my work from her. It frustrated her that I idled away my days doing unpaid work. She thought I would end up wasting my life.

"It is a sin to waste a life!" she screamed one day.

"I am not wasting my life; I do what no one else can do!" I said, then brought out artwork from underneath my bed and placed it before her.

One by one, she looked at each drawing until tears welled in her eyes. From that day on, she stopped pestering me. When she returned home every evening, she demanded to see my work. She looked, critiqued, and encouraged me to hone my skills and transform unfortunate people's lives into beautiful art. She began showing off my work to neighbors. Some expressed amazement at my God-given talent. A few disdained me for not being man enough to take care of my mother. I paid no heed; art consumed me.

One scorching hot afternoon, two men brought my mother's corpse home. Sunstroke had killed her. I was devastated. For months, I neglected my art, and with it, myself. I suffered alone. Everyone suffers, but each of us suffers in his own way.

Around this time, I turned eighteen and decided to sell my art on the street. I spread a dhurri on the busiest corner in my neighborhood. I sat on the dhurri, capturing the semblances of celebrities from their photographs—famous leaders, well-known personalities, Bollywood stars—and put them up for sale. My imitations drew people's attention. Passers-by stopped for a few minutes to watch me draw and paint.

"That is so lifelike!" a man said.

"God has blessed you with such a gift, son!" an elderly lady commented.

"Can you draw my face? I'll give you twenty rupees!" a young man asked.

"Twenty rupees, sir? Twenty rupees for all that work?" I said and stared hard at him.

"How much do you want?"

"Fifty?"

"Are you a conman or an artist?" he said. I ignored him and continued to draw.

"That line he just drew is worth twenty rupees!" someone shouted. "Give him what he is asking!"

"Why don't you get your picture made?" the first man said with irritation.

"If I had the money, I would!" the shouting man replied.

"What about thirty rupees?" the man asked.

"What about thirty-five?" I said, my heart beating fast.

That was my first. Soon after I raised my price to fifty, then seventy; soon, people were paying a hundred rupees to get their faces drawn. I made hundreds of faces—profile or full face, bust or full-length, monochromatic or full color.

A year after selling my first portrait, I installed a canvas canopy to protect me from rain and heat. I set a wooden table and comfortable chair beneath it. On another table, I displayed several portraits of famous people. Passersby took notice.

One day, as I was absorbed in sketching a scene, I heard someone say, "*O ladke*! Hey boy, this is not the way for a fine artist to work—like a beggar!" I looked up. A well-dressed older man had picked up a portrait and was examining it.

"Not a beggar, sahib! I am a painter of portraits," I said with pride.

The man introduced himself as Ravi Verma. He said for the last thirty years he had painted billboards advertising the Bollywood movies showing in the local cinema halls. However, he no longer had the energy of a young man to paint large works by himself. He needed an assistant. He offered me my first job; I was only too happy to accept.

Ravi Verma took me to his studio, which looked more like a warehouse. I was awed at the size of the heads and torsos and hands he drew on forty-by-thirty-foot canvases. They looked monumental compared to the eight-by-eleven or twelve-by-twenty-inch surfaces I drew on. My works seemed miniscule in comparison, and I couldn't wait to paint gigantic portraits.

Ravi Verma asked me to call him Vermaji. For the first few days, I observed him painting. He drew a grid on the white gesso surface that I helped prepare. He stood on scaffolding facing the canvas and drew ovals, circles, triangles, and rectangles until a composition of a group of people came alive—all whom I readily recognized as famous Bollywood stars. I watched as he transformed the two-dimensional surface into a three-dimensional scene. He brought familiar faces to life on screen-size canvases: heroines with almond eyes, luscious lips, and voluptuous busts and hips; heroes with handsome faces and dreamy eyes. His depiction of lanky or stocky villains, all with lecherous expressions, smoking cigarettes or holding glasses of whiskey amused me.

For the first few months as an apprentice, I was given the work of stretching raw canvas on wooden frames, applying gesso on the surfaces, and mixing and blending colors. In time, he let me fill in large areas with the appropriate flat paint. That did not require much skill, but it helped me gain confidence in working on large areas. After a day's work, I washed brushes and bowls and cleaned the floor splashed with multi-colored paint.

Within one year under Vermaji's supervision, I had learned to shade a chignon or show a curl on a heroine's forehead. Slowly, I learned how to paint ears, hands, and eyes and make them look real. Finally, I painted a face without his assistance.

The best day of my life was when he let me paint all the figures on a billboard. Upon examining the completed work, he said, "The student has become the master." I initially thought I had misunderstood, but from then on, he filled in the large surfaces with flat paint and I painted the figures and faces. I was ready for it. My skill and passion had been transformed into something much more than I had imagined. Full of energy, I painted with my whole body. Relieved to see that someone would continue his legacy, one day Vermaji said, "Your work vibrates with emotions. Hear me, son. You will go places."

Eventually, I began to get bored with painting the same faces over and over again. The excitement of copying famous Bollywood faces from photographs was gone, and I wanted to paint live models and make portraits with personality. I wanted to work independent of restraints and make vibrant and original portraits. I grew restless to leave, but did not want to disappoint the man who had supported me when I was nobody. I had developed affection for my employer. Would he get angry? Would he be sad? When I opened my heart to him, though, Vermaji understood my frustrations and my desires. He said he too was thinking of closing the business, of retiring. I thanked him for being my mentor, and we bid each other a sad but friendly good-bye.

Like the Bollywood stars that I had painted for five years, I dreamed about becoming rich and famous. I did not want to work in a warehouse; I wanted to work in a studio, have my own atelier. I did not want to live in an ordinary flat; I desired my own house. No, a mansion. I wanted to possess a motorbike. No, a car. I imagined a life of opulence and luxury.

Vermaji had given me the names and addresses of potential clients who were wealthy, and I introduced myself and showed them my portfolio. I looked covetously at their mansions and vehicles, and told myself, *All in good time, all in good time!*

Within days, I found my first patron, a director-producer with an unattractive face and manners but a very attractive purse. He was pleased with what I had done. No sooner had I finished that commission that my name spread wildly by word of mouth. I received so many jobs that I was kept occupied for a year. The more portraits I made, the more recognition I received. Although I exhibited my work in group shows, I had painted enough portraits for a solo exhibition. My patrons were glad to oblige me when I asked to borrow their portraits, especially when they learned that they would be displayed for other people to admire.

I first gained recognition at the local and state level, but then reviews of my shows began to appear in national newspapers. By the time I was in my late thirties, my deep driving desires had become reality. Art connoisseurs knew my name, and art admirers recognized my work. When the Ministry of Culture and Arts constructed an extension to their building, they asked me to paint four murals: Mahatma Gandhi, Rabindranath Tagore, Jawaharlal Nehru, and Indira Gandhi.

I painted the semblances of those great personalities, and I painted life-size images of city and suburban folks—suited and booted businessmen and local personalities looking smug as they posed; women decked in ornaments studded with gems modeled in their silk and chiffon saris; and children dressed in fashionable clothes sat restlessly to have their faces painted so as not to disappoint their eager parents.

The more paintings I made, the more famous I became. All the families in society's upper echelon wanted my portraits to adorn the drawing rooms of their mansions. I received more commissions than I could handle. My savings account was ballooning like a man who overeats. Was this the life I had wished for?

I met Shanti at the opening of one of my art shows. She was a writer and a lover of painting. She had accompanied her father, a real estate magnate, to my show. Before they left, he asked if I would paint a portrait of him and his daughter, and I agreed

I arrived at their home with my painting paraphernalia. They had selected a room, a chair, and a pose in which to have their image made. The father in a Nehru jacket and churidaar pajama, seated in an elaborately carved walnut seat, and the daughter standing next to him in a silk and brocade sari, decked in her late mother's gem-studded gold ornaments. I couldn't take my eyes off her. They posed for hours, the father's expression lost in thoughts and the daughter smiling intently at me with her dark almond-shaped eyes. Her presence inspired me to make one of my best works. The day I signed my name to their portrait, I asked her if she would marry me. She consented.

We honeymooned in the valley of Kashmir, and for the first several years returned there to holiday and celebrate our love. But gradually, our holiday time—I should say my holiday time—dwindled, and soon we stopped vacationing altogether. Why? Because I could not say no to new commissions. My work consumed me.

For the first several years, Shanti did not complain. She would spend a few weeks with her best friend Shakila, instead. More years flew by. By the fifth year, she begged me to take a break from my work, something she would have never done five years earlier. She suggested we take a few days away from my so-called "creating." I did not stop to think what she meant nor pay heed to the fact that she wanted my attention. I was obsessed, more with myself than my art. Unable to see my life from Shanti's perspective, I did not see myself. Money was pouring in, and I didn't see any reason to block its flow.

Fortunately, though, I did not ignore the cues and clues my body had begun to give me. I heard it telling me to STOP and breathe in the life that was passing so quickly by. My back ached a bit, and, at times my joints felt swollen and my legs more tired at the end of the day than they used to. Yet, at times, I pushed these signals aside I was still more concerned with how to delineate my clients' appearances with elegance and power than with paying attention to the message of an inner voice.

One fine spring evening, my wife and I were invited for dinner at the house of one of my old patrons, a businessman turned friend, Manoj Pathak. I had painted him, his wife, and their four children. The portraits hung in their living room and hallway. By now, painting silky black hair, black almond eyes, and beautiful skin had become second nature to me. I could paint a picture with my eyes closed—their creative significance and their uniqueness superficial, confined to their surfaces, as deep as the color pigment.

After enjoying a sumptuous dinner, we sat on their back porch to have hot masala tea.

"Life seems to be going quite well for you, young man!" the elderly businessman said as he patted my back. "You have everything a man dreams of! Could you imagine all this when you painted the billboards?"

"I couldn't! I'm fortunate!" I said. "Yet life seems to be flying by, don't you think?" I don't know why I said this to Manoj.

"Indeed! But we can't hold on to life, can we?" he said thoughtfully. "Anyway, I have something to tell you that should please you."

"Good news is always welcome!" I was eager to hear what he had to say.

"Recently, I had a chance to meet the Maharaja of Saurashtra. He was searching for a portrait painter. I told him about you and your extraordinary skill in painting exquisite portraits. He wants to get his and the maharani's portrait made."

"Oh!" I should have been thrilled. But I was not. "Thanks for your recommendation, but Ashok Patel, a young artist, is as good," I muttered.

"Of course he is! But this commission is for you, my dear friend. This is the opportunity of a lifetime!" He sounded more enthusiastic than me. "And the honorarium will be something you could only dream of." He moved, crossing his legs.

To my own surprise, I did not want to travel. I asked, "Is the maharaja planning a long stay and a trip to New Delhi? It would take me several weeks to paint a double portrait."

"Oh no! No, no! He is not planning to travel. Too much responsibility in his state, you know!" he said, giggling with pleasure.

"How does he expect me to paint his picture?"

"You have to go to Saurashtra." He narrowed his eyes.

At that moment, our wives joined us. Our host repeated to Shanti the maharaja's desire to have a double portrait painted. She said something about her own portrait with her father, and said, "At least this patron will take him away from his studio."

While driving back home, I asked Shanti if she thought I had traded my creative freedom for popularity and wealth. At first she did not respond. When I repeated my question, she said my asking that question meant I partly believed it.

"I don't know, but something from within is bubbling up, putting a doubt in my mind about my art," I blurted.

"I have been begging you to take a break, get away from it for a while. Perhaps this trip will do you good; you'll return refreshed and renewed. Perhaps you'll make something original."

"You think we should accept the maharaja's offer, then?" I looked expectantly at her.

"I don't know about the maharaja's offer, but going to Manipur Village in Saurashtra sounds like a good idea."

"How do you know about this village in Saurashtra?" I was glad to hear her excitement about visiting this place.

"Shakila has a cabin there. She talks about it all the time. It sounds like the most picturesque and mysterious town," she said. "There is magic in the air, Shakila says. Your mind will clear, your heart open, and your anxieties dissipate. Trust me, I feel it," Shanti said with her hand on her heart. "Perhaps we can spend some days in Shakila's cabin before you see the maharaja!"

"Why don't we stay in a hotel?" In a cabin? In some godforsaken village?

"Not a hotel, you'll love this place. So inspiring! Shakila spends a few months there every summer. She is not going this summer, though."

Having ignored my dear wife's wishes for so long, I couldn't say no to her.

It had been a month since the evening at the businessman's house. We left my atelier and our mansion behind. We traveled by train to the unfamiliar and unknown village that Shakila found magical and that had mesmerized my wife.

From Ahmadabad, we took a bus toward Manipur. We drove on unpaved paths through cornfields where stalks were ready for harvesting. Enclosed in husks, ripe yellow corn lay hidden behind silky golden hair. We crossed chili fields lush with the long pointed green leaves of red hot pepper plants. Our bus made one stop for passengers to use the latrines and step down to a historic well. Reaching into the water, we cupped our hands to drink and cool our parched throats, quench our thirst, and wash our faces.

Women in intricately embroidered backless cholis, blouses and brightly colored heavily pleated long skirts sold glass bangles and handmade trinkets. Their profiles were blurred behind muslin veils. In an open-air market, turbaned men majestic in their white kurtas and pajamas sold vegetables and fruit in circular baskets.

The bus dropped us at the edge of a vast field, and the only way to reach our destination was by bullock cart. We hired one, hopped in, and held our suitcases between our legs as the bullocks trotted off. The cart scurried along a rough path flanked by red pepper fields. Water-filled potholes splashed us, and the blue sky above blessed us.

At the edge of the pepper fields, the driver cried, "Ruk! Ruk!" and the bullocks halted. The driver asked us to jump out and stood to help us. I jumped out as he helped my wife down. With only a loincloth around his waist, I could see his ribs and shoulder blades. Exposed to the sun, the hue of his dark skin had intensified. I was reminded of my childhood when my mother and I had little to eat, just struggling to keep our body and soul together. He was the kind of man I used to paint. I tipped him more than his week's salary. He said if I liked he would wait for me as long as I wanted. He would drive us whenever and wherever we wanted to go. I thanked him but gently refused his offer.

A boy stood watching as the driver left, then walked closer to us.

"Do you know a caretaker by the name of Jaidev?" I asked. He nodded.

"Where is he?" Jaidev was to give us the key to Shakila's cabin. The boy nodded again and asked us to follow him. He led us away from the flaming expanse of pepper fields to a narrow lane before stopping in front of a mud hut. Then he disappeared as abruptly as he had appeared.

Shanti and I beheld the dramatic view of a solitary hut silhouetted under a large banyan tree. The rays of the setting sun haloed the dwelling. In the background, iridescent orange colored the western sky into a heavenly space. From where we stood, details were blurred, but a swing hanging on the front porch became visible. A circular window behind the swing mesmerized me, invited me in. I felt an urge to enter the hut. We walked toward the porch and ascended five steps. The swing creaked in the mild breeze.

Shanti, tired from the day's journey, settled on the swing to rest. I peered through the circular window and saw the interior of an unfurnished room, which I entered through the door. No smell. No color. Inside, on the front wall, I saw a blackened mirror hanging on a nail beneath an alcove. I picked it up. There was no reflection. Its black surface stared back at me. Then something uncanny happened. I felt uneasy, alone. I do not know why. I felt as if I had lost something. No, I had an urge to search for something, but did not know what I was supposed to find. Suddenly I felt as though I would amount to nothing until I found this nameless object.

I wanted to walk out and sit next to my wife. When I turned to leave, I saw an old man sitting in the corner of the room, behind the open door. Seated on a mat, he sat with his legs crossed. His hair was matted, his eyes half-closed, he had a beige shawl wrapped around his upper body. His left hand was placed over his left knee, the thumb touching his index finger. With his right hand, he was turning a rosary. Who was he? Jaidev's father?

"Namaskar, Babaji!" I greeted him. My voice croaked. I cleared my throat. Sitting still, he continued to turn the string of beads.

Feeling like an intruder, I did not want to disturb him more than I had.

The bitter smell of burnt rice drew me towards the kitchen. A pot of rice on the mud hearth had boiled over; it was dried and charred. The coal had turned to ash, and smoke seemed to escape through the window above the hearth. It left a lingering odor. The sunlight reflected upon the still life, and I paused. Making a viewfinder by crossing two fingers of my two hands and looking through it, I slowly pivoted on my heels with my knees gently bent. I stopped at different positions when my finger-frame focused on an appealing view. Compositions of white, black, gray, and orange-gold surfaced in my consciousness. The evening light glistened on the pots and pans as it brushed their surfaces; the sheen of highlights contrasted with dark kitchen nooks. My creative instincts gushed. How I wished I had my canvas and paints. But the burnt odor drew me back to the present.

I stepped from the kitchen to the porch. In the silence I heard water dripping from a faucet at the other end of the hut from where Shanti rested. Seeing her eyes closed, I tiptoed toward the drip. The water had filled a tin bucket that now overflowed. I tightened the faucet and returned to sit on the swing at the small space left near my wife's feet. The swing creaked and woke her up.

"Did you get the keys?" she asked with her eyes closed.

"Not yet." I could not get the image of the blackened mirror out of my mind.

"Didn't you find the caretaker?" She raised her head, her eyes half-closed.

"I will. Shanti, I feel something in this house… something I cannot describe…something...."

"What are you talking about?" She sat up.

"I found a blackened mirror that I can't get out of my mind. A man is meditating in that room. Something in there is calling me back. Stay here until I return."

I walked back into the room. The old man's eyes were still closed. I walked to the alcove and picked up the mirror. I needed to see my face, but it wasn't there. What could this be? Black paint? Soot? I pulled my monogrammed white handkerchief from my pocket and used spit to rub the surface of the mirror, first mildly, then frantically. Slowly, the gunk and grime came off. I walked to the water faucet, wet the soiled handkerchief, and again rubbed the surface until it glistened. In the process of cleaning the mirror, the handkerchief turned into a dirty rag.

I walked back to the room with the mirror in my hand. From the window I saw Shanti pacing outside the hut. I looked at my reflection. It looked back at me, pierced me with its gaze. *Who are you?* A soundless voice startled me. It was as if I was looking at myself for the first time. At that moment, someone's presence startled me.

"It scared you, didn't it?" Babaji stood in front of me.

"What did?" I asked, aghast.

"The dark mirror!" Babaji smiled. "I too was unable to see my true reflection—inward. I must have been your age then . . . it was years ago . . . when I saw my Self."

"Why is it that since I found this mirror I have felt confused, disintegrated?" I was desperate to know, and Babaji asked me to sit down. We sat cross-legged on the floor facing each other. He asked me about myself, and I gave him the highlights of my life while he listened attentively.

"As a child, dear son, you were your authentic Self. But as you grew older, your desire for power, possessions, and position increased. You showed only your masked face to the world, even to your Self. So much so that you began to see your Self as others saw you—with a mask. Your authentic Self, thus neglected, went dormant."

"I don't remember losing touch with my Self. When did I put on the mask?" I asked.

"When you became disconnected from your heart. When you started to paint semblances of people. When instead of expressing your deep-seated urge to paint the human condition, you started to decorate surfaces. You got disconnected from your heart, your soul. This is your story, my story, the story of everyone, whether you are professionally successful or unsuccessful, rich or poor. Ultimately, each one of us at some point in our lives must face the emptiness of our masked Selves and search for our authentic Self."

Babaji continued: "Many years ago, I tried to look at my own reflection. Hidden behind it, I saw someone else. Who was it whose heart beat in unison with mine? Was someone else beside me living within, equally engaged in my daily affairs? But I did not pay attention. Who was it that wore the clothes I wore, lived in my house, witnessed my thoughts, actions, words, watched over me, and when I was at crossroads, nudged me in the right direction? But I paid no heed; worldly affairs devoured me. I was enticed by pretense while my divine Self loved me from within."

At that moment, I felt charged with the same flow that used to pass through me when I was inspired. Long ago, it had directed me, taken pleasure in my work, and been my constant companion. Now I was controlled by outer circumstances. I was told what to do and when to do it. The quicksand of success had made me forget who I really was. I had let the dazzle of fame eclipse the light of my inspiration, the light of my life.

From the window, I saw Shanti attentively listening to a man. Before hanging the mirror back on the wall, I turned to thank Babaji, but he was gone. I was alone in the room. His sudden disappearance jolted me. But I grounded myself and hung the mirror where I had found it. I walked back slowly to where my wife was.

"This is Jaidev, the caretaker," my wife said.

"Sorry for the inconvenience sir! Someone directed you to an abandoned house. Please follow me to my office. I'll hand you the keys to your cabin."

"Abandoned?"

"Yes sir. Nobody has lived here in years. Some people even believe it is haunted. Please come."

I held Shanti's warm hand and squeezed it gently. She smiled back at me. We quietly followed Jaidev. As I stopped momentarily to take another look at the house, my earlier life reeled through my mind.

THE THUG

"I wonder what happened to Mahadeo's wife?" Brij said half to himself and half to me as he sipped his evening tea. I was peeling potatoes to fry. The aroma of steaming rice filled the kitchen.

"You still don't believe me?" I said as I tossed the potatoes into the sizzling mustard oil. "He killed her. May Lord Shiva protect me for saying this, but I think he is a villain. He killed her! Otherwise, where did she disappear to?"

"Why do you keep saying that?" Brij hit the table with his fist, frustrated at how many times I had repeated this accusation.

"Everyone says he murdered his wife!"

"Do they have proof? Bah, murder! I keep telling you this man is not capable of such a thing. You and your friends can have your fun, but soon this gossip will fade—until you have something else to talk about." His voice lowered as he looked away through the window.

"You wouldn't say that about Mahadeo if I told you what happened to Radha last week." I ignored his comment about gossip and waved the steel spatula in front of his face. "Mahadeo badgered her."

"Who, Radha Kichlu?"

"Yes, her." I turned around and added fresh peas to the pot. With my back facing him, I told him how Mahadeo had harassed Radha as she bathed in the river.

"Nonsense . . . rumors, just rumors!"

"Well, rumor has it he roams the streets at night like a thug and a bully."

"And you trust Radha? The seductress? I wouldn't be surprised if you said that she harassed *him*!" Brij retorted. I gently hit my husband on the shoulder.

"I have known Mahadeo as a good-hearted fellow. In high school, he was a prankster, funny but simple. And I have never heard any complaints from his co-workers at the papier-mâché factory. He was a good friend of mine until recently. Thanks to your gossip, he keeps to himself."

"Where did his wife vanish to then, han? I don't know why you keep defending that monster. He is a thug, I tell you, and should be behind bars," I said as I busied myself making dinner. Why wasn't my husband on my side? I was so frustrated! No matter what I said, I failed to convince him.

The next morning, I jumped out of bed. It was time to go to the temple. Brij was snoring, his head turned towards the wall. I walked to the window and looked at the sky. The sun would rise in half an hour or so, but the morning was overcast. I splashed my face with water, rolled my long black hair into a chignon, and wrapped myself in a crisp yellow sari. After collecting a brass tumbler from the puja room, I went downstairs and put on my sandals. I stepped outside into stark silence and closed the front door behind me. The clouds had turned darker and denser. The bark of a dog made me feel uneasy. Usually at this time, a chorus of birds greeted me. Where were they? No one was up and about, but they would be soon, I told myself as I crossed the lane that joined the paved road. I looked up and hoped it wouldn't rain. Muttering the mantra *aum . . . aum . . . aum*, I headed to the temple of Lord Krishna.

At the temple, where the cobblestones surrounding the building extended to where the steps began, I turned left and stepped down to the riverfront. I placed the tumbler beside me, and tucking my sari between my legs, squatted to do morning ablutions. I then filled the tumbler with fresh water to offer the gods. Why had the other worshippers not arrived yet? Was it some kind of holiday? I usually greeted a number of people on the riverfront, but no one was in sight today. My heart started to beat fast. As I walked up the steps, the silhouette of the temple on the hill—black against the blue-black sky—came into view. A figure stood against the front railing that led to the main temple gate. At least one person had arrived. As I neared the gate, the figure revealed itself to be a man. His cigarette glowed neon red, blinking off as he took long puffs. When he walked towards me, my heart skipped a beat.

"Lady, what are you doing here at this hour?" He threw the cigarette butt on the ground, crushing it underfoot.

"Why do you ask? I come here every day at this time!" I nervously cleared my throat.

"You come here this early, at three in the morning? It is not safe for a woman to be out by herself at this time. Thugs and all, you know."

"Three!" I gasped. "I thought it was much later, like five."

A bolt of lightning lit the sky. In that brief flash of light, I saw the man's dark pants and shirt, his disheveled black hair, and his thick mustache. He had a grin on his face.

I turned around and began to take long strides towards home. The sprinkle of rain swelled to a shower. My sandals kept getting stuck in the cobblestone crevices. I took them off and held them in one hand, turned the tumbler upside down, and ran. I heard him calling me by my name, "Stop, Lakshmi! Don't be afraid!"

How does he know who I am? I was afraid for my life. "Go away!" I screamed. "I have nothing valuable on me!"

He shouted something I did not understand. Fear turned me senseless, and I slipped and fell. I managed to get up, but the pleats of my sari came undone, entangling under my feet and making me fall again. I gathered the sari in my arms, holding it together with my hands. With only blouse and petticoat covering my body, from the corner of my eye, I saw the man behind me. I got up and began to run again.

"Please wait!" the man said. "You're getting wet." He flipped open the umbrella he was carrying. "Use this!" he said and extended it to me.

"My husband will be here soon," I said.

"Why don't you fix your sari? I'll hold up the umbrella," he continued as if he had not heard what I said.

He held the large umbrella over my head and turned around to look the other way.

I retied my sari.

"Here are your tumbler and sandals. You dropped them on the road."

In the frenzy of fear, I had forgotten about what I had been holding when I tried to fix my sari. Wet and shivering with fear, I took my things. The man removed his coat and wrapped it around my shoulders.

"I don't think you recognize me," he said. "I'm Mahadeo."

"Maa . . . haa . . . deo!" I could hardly breathe. Whether it was the amazement of this chance meeting with him or the shame of gossiping about him, I did not know.

"Yes, Mahadeo. I know Brij. We are—were school friends."

I did not know what to say to this man whose name I had maligned. We walked in silence, listening to the thunder and pouring rain.

"The things people say about you, are they true?" I finally asked.

"What do people say?"

"That you killed your wife."

"What do I care about what people say?"

"Why would people say a thing like that?"

"I don't know. Vicious minds attract vicious thoughts."

"She couldn't have just disappeared, could she?"

"She ran away."

"What!" I stopped and turned to look at him.

"I did not kill her or drive her away. She ran away with another man."

"She ran away? Where? With whom?" I had never felt so shamed as I did at that moment.

"To Goa, with a cousin of mine." He sounded sad.

"People say—" I started.

"Do you believe all the things people say? You should not!"

"I should have believed my husband. He defended you all along." We continued to walk toward my home.

"What did he say?"

"He said you are an honorable man, that you were a funny prankster in school, and honest."

"What else did he say?" I heard a smile in his voice.

"He said he hates gossip and those who spread rumors."

"What reason did you have not to agree with him?"

I did not know how to truthfully answer his question, so I changed the subject. I said, "He misses you! He wonders why you have stopped seeing him. Why don't you let people know what you just told me?"

"Why is it anybody's business? Besides, my wife rejected my love. I was too dejected to defend myself. My wife dishonored me. She hurt my pride. It pained me to realize that while I loved her, she loved someone else."

"I am so sorry about what happened." My feelings for a person had never changed as quickly as they did about him.

"You can't force someone to love you."

Not knowing what to say, I changed the subject again and said, "Why have you been avoiding your friends? My husband?"

"They may have misread my pain as avoidance. People think life revolves around them. I was taking care of my pain. They could have stepped up and offered to help."

We had reached the narrow lane that led to my house.

"But why—you knew all along who I was? What were you doing at the temple this early?"

"I work the nightshift. The factory had a power failure. They let us out early. I was on my way home. Anyway, give my best to Brij," Mahadeo said.

I bid him good-bye at the front door, walked through the foyer, and climbed the stairs. My husband was still sleeping. I removed my sari, and without changing my petticoat or blouse, laid next to him. It was still dark, but the rain had stopped.

In the distance, I heard the temple bells chime and thought of the man who loved his wife, even though she left him for someone else; the man whose peace of mind had been stolen by rumors and gossip; the lonely, honorable man who I had called a thug.

A PRECIOUS GIFT

My things were packed: one faux leather suitcase, one yellow duffel bag, and one genuine leather purse. I was ready to leave for the train station. My parent's home was in the valley of Kashmir, and we lived in the city of Belgaum, in the southern state of Karnataka—a three-day journey by train. I should have been excited, as I always was before visits to my childhood home; instead, I was somber and nervous. I was going to see my mother almost a year after my father's death. I had been unable to attend the thirteen-day death ceremonies presided over by my uncle. My husband, Aakash, had been sick. At first his doctor was unable to pinpoint the problem and diagnosed it as leukemia. After six months of treatment, we consulted another doctor, who confirmed that instead of leukemia, Aakash had an infection of the immune system. The medication cured him in a few months, but before I could leave him alone again, ten months had passed.

The phone rang, pulling me back to the present.

"Auntie!" It was Suraj, our son Shubh's best friend. "Shubh was in a car accident," he sobbed.

"When? Where? Is he all right?" My legs felt weak; my mind darted in a million different directions.

Suraj did not answer.

"Are you there? Suraj, where is Shubh? Where are you?"

Again, there was silence on the other end.

"Suraj! Suraj, it's all right. Tell me which hospital did they take him to?" I so badly wanted him to answer.

"He did not . . . they could not . . ." His words were broken by sobs.

"What did he not? Who are they? Is he badly hurt?" Limb by limb, my body went numb.

"No, Auntie, he is no longer with us," he managed to say.

"No, this can't be true! You must have heard it wrong." My mind did not want to process his words and make them real.

"We are at the hospital. I am with him. Please come!" I heard him loud and clear before he hung up.

This can't be true. Oh, my baby, my only baby! My Shubh! My life! I fell, my elbow hitting the floor with a thud. Piercing pain shot up through my elbow to my wrist and fingertips. Such a careful driver! No longer with us? DEAD! The meaning of the words exploded in my brain.

I lay flat on the bed, my brain foggy and my eyelids heavy, as if small stones lay on them, my arms and legs leaden with weights. I tried to open my eyes, tried to sit up, but was unable to. Where was I? Why was I in such agony, my heart so heavy? I had a nightmare. I shrieked so loud that it pierced all six cosmic directions. The echo brought Aakash running to my room. He sat on my bed, wiped away my tears with his thumbs and caressed my cheeks.

"I had a nightmare, Aakash; it was horrible . . . just horrible," I moaned. My arms crossed against my chest, I looked at the ceiling. "Where is our Shubh? Tell me, where is he?"

He stroked my hair and kissed me on my forehead, tears welling in his puffy eyes. He slid to the edge of our bed and put my feet on his thighs. He warmed his palms together and rubbed the soles of my cold feet. Then he massaged my legs. He had never done that before. There had been no need.

"It was awful, Aakash, just awful. I dreamed we were in a funeral home. And we let our baby . . . oh, the flames . . . the furnace!" I cried.

"Shhh . . . you didn't dream it, Sheela!" he sobbed.

I turned away from him as if our son's death had been his doing. I lay in a fetal position, my palms pressed together between my knees. "In minutes, he was gone! Why did you let him burn? Why didn't they burn me instead? Where did he go? Where is he now?" So restless, so listless, I turned to face him. "He was with us yesterday. Where is he today?" He didn't answer.

I lay flat, looking at the ceiling. Aakash left. My arms stretched over my head, and with fingers spread, I screamed. "Tell me . . . please, please, somebody tell me it is not true . . ." I cried. I sobbed. I would have done anything to be rid of the black mass pressing against my chest.

Aakash returned with a glass of water and a white tablet. He handed me the glass and said, "Please take a sedative. It'll help you sleep." I did not refuse. I gulped the tablet down with sips of water.

I floated in and out of sleep. The neon letters of the electric clock glared 3:20 a.m. My mouth felt bitter. I could not go back to sleep, but I was determined to keep my eyes shut until dawn. It seemed like an eternity. When would this darkness end? But our son had died—how could there ever be light again? When I opened my eyes. It was 3:30 a.m. Time had almost come to standstill. Stopped. We all might as well die. When I opened my eyes again, the risen sun was hiding behind indigo-black clouds.

I did not want to see anyone, talk to anyone, visit anyone. Isolated from others, I could be with Shubh. Shubh's memories kept me company. Aakash's colleagues at the university came to extend their condolences. He sat with them in the living room, talking softly. They tried consoling him but were afraid to further upset me. They left, unable to soothe him or reassure me. Our uninvited sorrow and pain was there to stay.

Misunderstandings or resentments I had with the world seemed petty. They drowned in the depth of my inner abyss, also the source of my pain, fear, and guilt. I had lost everything. My life seemed to have no purpose.

There were days when I heard my husband crying in the next room, the volume turned on the television or classical music turned high to hide it from me. Soon he resumed his teaching routine. Someone had to earn money for life's necessities.

For weeks, I watched him courageously restart his life. I tried to get back to my own daily routine, but my mind was bombarded with memories of Shubh: his face, his voice, his laughter.

My movements had slowed to that of a caterpillar, as if I were sick or frail or at the verge of death. With all my physical energy drained, it was as though vitality had been sucked out of me. Doing tasks as ordinary as making a cup of tea was hard to do, and drinking it more like a burden. I was unable to free myself of indolence or be rid of the thick clouds that covered my mind. Some days I started to feel better, but would sink back into the whirlpool of helplessness and hopelessness.

One day, while sitting at the kitchen table, I stared at the wall, daydreaming of what it would have been like if Shubh had lived to be twenty or forty or sixty years old. I could not and felt frustrated.

"Don't forget to have your breakfast!" Aakash said before leaving for the university. "Today, I may come home early. If I don't, I'll call you." He kissed me on top of my head and left, and I heard the front door close behind him.

I sat at the table for a long time, then forced myself to make a cup of tea. I boiled water. Put a teaspoon of Darjeeling leaves into the white ceramic pot Shubh gave us for our twentieth wedding anniversary. I poured boiling water over the leaves, put on the lid, and placed my cold palms around the belly of the pot. Shubh's smile reeled before me. I saw him watching as I opened the red box tied with a silver ribbon and take out the white ceramic teapot. Then his image disappeared.

Why won't the earth split asunder and take me into its boiling lava? Please, God, please help me. Burn my body and help me disappear into oblivion!

Insanity consumed me. Obsession fogged my mind. Not a thing was as it had been. Why did it have to change? Why was he snatched from us? I picked up the teapot and hurled it against the wall. It fell to the floor with a crash, the ceramic pieces scattering and pale streaks of tea dripping down with a few tealeaves still stuck to the wall.

I realized what I had done. "Shubh, oh, Shubh, where are you? Where are you, my baby?" I crouched on the wet floor and cried. I put my arms around my knees and rolled back and forth, back and forth, back and forth.

I heard my husband let himself in. I was fearful of upsetting him. I understood why he felt the way he did about me, but I was unable to bounce back like him. I tried to get up.

"I'm home," he said as he came through the front door. At the kitchen entrance, he halted. "What happened here?" he said, his brows furrowed and mouth open.

I got up, my pajamas still wet from the spilled tea.

"What happened, Sheela?" he asked again. "Goddamn it! What's wrong with you?" he said, spit spewing from his mouth, "Th- this d-death, this t-tragedy has taken its toll on me too. But you don't see me brooding, unkempt, lying in filth." I got up. He tore several sheets from a roll of paper towels. "Snap out of it!" he yelled, and let the towels absorb the liquid on the floor. I stepped back as he came closer to where I was standing. I stood still against the wall and guiltily watched him clean up my mess. He gathered the pieces of ceramic and dumped them in the garbage can. He brought the broom from the laundry closet, swept and mopped the floor, and wiped the wall clean. He washed and dried his hands at the basin.

He walked toward me, stood still, and stared at me. Then he held my shoulders with his hands and kissed my forehead, my eyes, my cheeks, my lips. All I could see was Shubh, laughing, calling, singing, crying. How much he looked like his father!

"Do you hear him, do you see our son?" I whispered. He shook his head, holding me tight and putting his cheek against mine.

"I do, I do! But if we lose touch with reality, we'll go mad, Sheela!"

I began to sob. "I feel so guilty, so guilty. I didn't do a thing to save him!"

"What could you have possibly done? He was not with you! Why would you feel guilty?"

"I don't know."

"Do you think we should get professional help?" he asked tentatively, afraid I might misunderstand his suggestion.

"No, I'll push myself to get better. I know I'm driving you crazy, but I just can't get him out of my mind." I pressed the sides of my forehead with my fingers.

"Take it one day at a time. Trust me, you will feel better. It will take its own time. You may not believe it, but you will feel better."

"I don't know. For your sake, Aakash, I hope so."

"Why don't you visit your mother as you had planned?" He held my cold hands between his warm palms.

"What about you?"

"I have my job. My students keep me occupied. It seems harder for you to cope. Think about it, take your time, and then decide." For those few moments, as I stood facing my husband, for the first time in months, the weight pressing against my chest lightened.

"Now please get into dry clothes. I'll make lunch."

I wanted to alleviate my pain to some level, but I was not yet ready to visit my mother. The only thing I had left of Shubh were memories, I decided to make an album of his photographs. I gathered all our pictures, black and white, colored, loose, and the ones pasted in three old albums. One by one, I looked at them and separated my favorite ones and added the ones Aakash loved. Shubh with a pacifier in his mouth; Shubh crawling in the living room of our first flat at the University of Kashmir; Shubh as a two-year-old in my mother's lap; Shubh in a blue-and-white checkered shirt in his kindergarten class; the first day of primary school; with his father in middle school; laughing at his high school graduation.

I purchased an album with a white cover and gold border. Everyday after Aakash left for work, I lost myself in the world when Shubh was with us. Arranging the photographs on an album pages, I decorated each page with colored designs: white of snow, green of spring grass, navy blue of the starlit sky—Shubh's favorite colors. The day the album was finished, I was ready to visit my mother.

I planned to spend two restful weeks in the house I was born in. My seventy-five-year-old mother lived in a two-story wood-and-mud house. The back faced east and overlooked the River Jehlum.

Underneath the second floor deck, she had planted a patch of garden that was in full bloom. She had planted flowers: marigold in various hues of gold, mustard, and cadmium yellow, roses, and lilies. She had also planted mint and coriander, green chili peppers and daikon radishes. It surprised me because she had never been a gardener. It was relaxing, she said, as much as reading books. She had started the garden patch after her husband's death.

Every day after dinner, we drank tea on the deck—an extension of the second-story family room with a view of the river. It became a ritual, a formal recognition of the end of a good day, the promise of another sunrise. Together, we looked at the river and listened to the water that had flowed since primordial times and would continue until eternity. I was grateful for this time together with my mother; it helped to mourn in the very house in which we had lived as a family.

During our time together, we talked about my father and Shubh. We had talked on the telephone and in our letters, but sitting with her on the deck sipping tea, I felt an intimate connection that healed. I talked and she listened. She consoled the way only a mother would: pressing my hand, rubbing my back, listening without commenting, then advising but not judging.

Having lightened my burden, a calm came over me.

The day before I was to leave, my mother and I sat as usual on the deck after dinner. The moon was full. Its silver sheen made me feel at one with everything: my mother, the house, the river, and the vast indigo-blue sky. Moonbeams rippled silver on the surface of the waves below. Silence filled the air. We sipped sweet chai and listened to the river flow.

Each time she mentioned Shubh or my father, tears sprang to my eyes. I had not really mourned for Shubh nor expunged the sorrow of my father's death. After Shubh, the loss of my father seemed an easier burden.

In my last conversation with my father, he told me about the significance of self-sufficiency, how being strong within strengthens other relationships as well. My mother seemed to have absorbed that lesson. I thought, as a new widow, it would be hard for her to live alone. But she had adjusted. Perhaps better than when my father was alive. She took care of herself and the house, and her face reflected equanimity and peace. Was she as sorrowful as I? How could one compare sorrows? Each one of us has his or her own way of dealing with the pain of separation and death. How much did she miss her husband's company? How did she manage to live alone day after day? What did she think of death?

"I was never as awed by God as I was when your father died. 'Where did he go?' I asked myself," my mother said. "Imagine a person alive for fifty, sixty, seventy years—breathing, talking, eating, laughing, feeling, thinking, sitting next to you, and then, in an instant, gone, disappeared."

After he passed away, my mother said she felt his absence; the spaces he used to occupy were empty. That depressed her, causing her to be disinterested in worldly things. But she pulled herself up and started to go for regular morning walks. Surrounded by nature, she said, the long walks helped her wake up to the world again. Sitting still at a clearing in the woods with nothing but birdcalls and swishing leaves on the branches of trees transported her into repose. Before his death, she had not walked for the sake of walking, nor had she gardened.

She looked up at the sky. "Moonlit nights remind me of your father—I feel connected to him by looking at the full moon." Her gray hair was tied up in a chignon, her crisp, starched sari neatly wrapped, its pallu falling gracefully behind her left shoulder. Twin moons reflected in her pupils.

"Mama, don't you feel lonely?"

"At first, child, I was in a daze. A cold emptiness overcame me. But I did not let it make me suffer. I felt it and let it pass through me. I neither ignored it nor suppressed it. Just walked with it. In time, the feeling dissolved. I let fine memories surface and remain, the good times we had together."

"What do you think happens when we die?" I asked.

"I don't know. One cannot think about these things; one can only feel them. As you know, I have witnessed many deaths. And after your father's passing, I came to realize that death is to life what night is to day; one has no reality without the other."

"Do you mean that in death we become what we were before birth?"

"No, dear, I am not saying that, although that, too, makes sense. What I am saying is we must not focus on the fact that we die but on the fact that we live. As human beings, there is nothing more encouraging than knowing we have the ability to make choices at every moment. It is up to us to choose how to live and to know that life is a gift, a precious gift. This is a fact irrespective of the intensity and type of suffering we undergo. People go away, pass on, change, and we are left behind."

Mama's voice was coming from deep inside her, and she continued, "The secret is to always keep in mind that death walks by our side. But most of us forget this and indulge in foolish and harmful things that waste our time. If we keep death in our mind, every minute becomes precious," she said. "My dear, know this secret and accept every single day as if it is gift from God. The way we live determines the way we die."

"What are you saying? Did Shubh not live well, then?"

"No, not at all! I don't know why some die young or some are born sick, or why there are a hundred different ways people suffer. But billions of us who live long lives tend to forget the secret. If we pay attention to the fact that death is our companion, it makes life a precious gift and our living meaningful. Each human life has a purpose."

"What is the purpose of my life, Mama? How does one know?" I blurted.

"Ask yourself. Ask the divinity that dwells within you what the purpose of your life is. In the depth of silence, listen to yourself; you will get your answer."

Moonlight reflected on Mama's gentle face, bestowing it with divine grace.

The next day I left with a new hope in my heart, to begin my life with Aakash anew. Together, we were stronger. One and one make eleven, my mother always said. The following year, she passed away. I let my heart ache. In time, my sorrow passed. Good memories of my last days with her were with me. I basked in those memories, keeping in mind my constant companion and focusing on the preciousness of our lives.

A CHANCE MEETING

Two winters ago, my general manager, Mr. Mehra, instructed me to represent our drug manufacturing company, Ayurveda Drugs, at the Annual International Pharmaceutical Conference in my city, New Delhi.

The first morning of the conference, I sat next to a Japanese delegate. The day started with a welcome greeting followed by a talk about a new drug for Alzheimer's made from an amalgamation of Indian turmeric roots and other chemicals. I attentively followed the talk that included diagrams and images of the human brain pre- and post-disease. Hours passed quickly, and it was time to stretch our legs. I got up, as did the Japanese delegate. He turned to me and smiled. I folded my palms and introduced myself. "I'm Mohan Bhargav." He introduced himself as Tetsu Ishadate and bowed low, giving me a glimpse of his salt-and-pepper hair. About five feet tall, he seemed to be in his late sixties. I asked him if this was his first trip to India. In broken English, he said he had been to India twice. He had visited

Mumbai, Bangalore, and Calcutta but had never been to New Delhi.

At lunch, I saw Tetsu Ishadate seated with some delegates from other countries, and I asked if I could join them. He pointed to an empty chair next to him, and I sat down. He savored each dish that was served, asking its Hindi name and if I thought it was tasty.

"Paneer pulao, aloo chole, gobi, et cetera. Not as tasty as homemade," I said.

"Are you good cook?" someone from the group asked.

"Not me, but my mother is."

During our lunch conversations, I discovered that Ishadate was keen on Indian architecture and interested in seeing local monuments. He said he planned to stay an extra day to visit local historic places. He also wanted to know about my work and family. I told him that I had been working for my current employer since my graduation from Delhi University five years earlier, and that recently I had purchased a two-bedroom flat where I lived with my mother. As we ate, several other Japanese delegates came over to say hello and greeted him as Professor Ishadate.

On the second day of the conference, I again exchanged greetings with the professor. I asked him if he slept well. He said yes, and that he felt well rested and was ready to hear more about groundbreaking research and innovative drugs being introduced into the market. The day was similar to the previous one, informative and positively affirming about the future of pharmaceutical companies. New information and methodologies about drugs that claimed to cure diseases overwhelmed me. I made meticulous notes because I would be required to present to Mr. Mehra what I'd learned.

At the end of that day, Professor Ishadate asked if I could recommend a tour guide to show him New Delhi's historic sites on his last day in India.

"But you can't see everything in one day," I exclaimed.

"Only important buildings," he said. "Next time, visit more."

"What about evenings? You have three evenings—visit one monument each evening, and on the last day, see the remaining ones. That way, you could fit in all the important sites within the time you have."

"Hmm—tour guide meet me in the evenings?"

"Don't worry about the tour guide; I'll take you around." For some reason, I felt like spending more time with him.

He was taken aback. "Thank you, but no trouble for you!"

"No trouble at all! How many times in my life would I get a chance to be a Japanese professor's tour guide?"

"Yah . . . yah . . . thank you very much!" He bowed several times and laughed heartily.

For the next three evenings, the professor sat on the backseat of my Honda scooter as I drove him to see the local historic monuments. It was June and the temperature hovered between one hundred five and one hundred ten degrees Fahrenheit. Although the evenings were a few degrees cooler, the hot wind blew our hair and the sun scorched our scalps as we rode the Honda.

The first evening I drove him to Qutab Minar, the second-tallest freestanding tower in India. It was constructed in 1192 with red sandstone and inlaid with white sandstone decorations. Looking up at the tower from the ground, the professor admired its outer wall decorated in arabesque style with quotes from the Quran.

"Very, very, elegant!" he said. He took pictures and was impressed by how the wide base of Qutab Minar narrowed at the top. Then, together, we climbed the 379 spiraling stairs to the top of the tower. For his age, he ascended energetically to the top. From a height of 240 feet, we admired South Delhi, which looked like a Lilliputian city.

The second evening I drove him to Humayun's Tomb, the first garden-tomb of a Mughal emperor. Designed by a Persian architect, it was commissioned by Humayun's widow, Empress Bega Begum, in 1569. Ishadate pointed out that the exclusive use of red sandstone gave the monument an aristocratic look, and yet its geometric symmetry imparted serenity. I translated signs and boards written in Hindi for him, and in return, I received lessons in aesthetics. Our sightseeing together seemed like a good bargain.

After only two evenings with Ishadate, I felt as if our acquaintance had developed into a friendship. I offered to treat the professor to sugarcane juice, a local drink, and he agreed. At the street vendor's stall, he drank a few sips to please me, but I could see that he did not like it. Too sweet for the Japanese, who do not include desserts with their meals, I supposed. So I drove him to a place where green coconuts were sold. He took a sip, said it was refreshing, and relished its flavor. Then he half-joked that a spicy meal following that drink would be most enjoyable.

"I didn't think you would like spicy food."

"Why?" He raised his brows.

"Because Japanese food is so mild."

"Reason I like spicy," he said.

On the third and last evening, we went to Jantar Mantar Park, a Hindu monument with thirteen monumental astronomical instruments. Built by a Hindu maharaja, Jai Singh II, in 1724, the primary purpose of the observatory was to compile astronomical tables and to predict the movements of the sun, moon, and planets. Professor Ishadate made me pose in front of Samrat Yantra, a sundial seventy feet high, one hundred fourteen feet long, and ten feet thick. He wanted to photograph its 128-foot-long hypotenuse, which parallels the earth's axis and points towards the North Pole. Then we posed together and let a passerby take our picture.

We made our way to Misra Yantra, the monument that determines the shortest and longest days of the year. It indicates the exact moment noon occurs in various cities and locations, regardless of their distance from New Delhi. "Remarkable, quite remarkable," he said and asked me to take his picture in front of it.

His keen interest in Indian architecture and admiration for the monuments we visited made me ask him about Japanese Zen temples. I had glanced at them in books and had been intrigued by the Zen gardener's ability to merge his skill with nature, how the natural beauty was maintained and manicured for a unique aesthetic.

"Nature and gardener come together," he said.

Did he mean that the gardener skillfully cultivated natural beauty? I asked, and he agreed. Were they gardens or temples, I also wanted to know. He said they were the places where time stopped. "Me and nature, one," he said. "Harmony between people and nature. Walk in garden, drink tea." He looked at my confused expression, and added, "You visit garden and know better!" I could not experience Zen gardens by listening to him. Perhaps, someday during my lifetime, I might visit Kyoto and Tokyo and walk through one, I thought.

It was late in the evening, and we were hungry. "Why don't we go to a dhaba? You like spicy food," I suggested.

"What is dhaba?"

"A roadside eatery. The one I want to take you to is known for its gol gappas."

"Gul goppas?"

"Gol gappa! It is a hollow, crispy dough sphere the size of a golf ball. Very light. You pierce a hole at the top." I made a gesture of holding the ball with my left hand and pointed my right finger at its top. "You fill it with spicy liquid and eat it. Very spicy!"

"Good! Okay we go," he said with a glint in his eyes.

We drove to a dhaba in Safdarjung market, famous for its gol gappas. The seller sat cross-legged under a canopy on a wooden platform. In front of him were two earthenware vessels three feet in circumference. At this cooler part of the day, we were the only customers there. After welcoming us, the seller handed each of us a paper plate, grabbed a gol gappa from a mound of balls in a large wicker basket, pierced it with his finger, dropped in a few chick peas, filled it with the sweet lemony-peppery juice from one of the vessels, and served the mouthwatering ball first to our Japanese guest and then to me.

The professor watched as I crunched the crispy ball in my mouth and gulped it down. Then he slugged his down too. The taste exploded in his mouth, and his eyes widened, his lips stretched, and he sucked in air. But he did not say, "No more, thanks!" Instead, he extended his plate for another and another and another. He kept gulping and sucking air, smiling all the while. We ate, sucked air, and smiled a dozen times until sweat beaded on our foreheads. The seller filled the thirteenth gol gappa with chickpeas and spicy liquid and offered it to the professor. But he shook his head, kept his plate on the side table, and patted his belly. "Very tasty!" he complimented him. I paid gol gappa wala a little more than what we owed him for the two-dozen balls of heaven.

"Very tasty! Funny to eat!" the professor said as we drove back to his hotel.

Since I had been taking Professor Ishadate sightseeing each evening, I told my mother that on the last day I might bring him home for dinner.

Ishadate wanted to buy gifts for his family, so on the extra day he'd added to his stay in New Delhi, his last in the city, I drove him to Connaught Place, the most vibrant business district of New Delhi. I parked my Honda scooter in CPs outer circle, and we crossed the road to the inner circle. With each store's best wares displayed in bay windows, we window-shopped under a canopied path, and the professor looked for gifts that would interest his family.

As we strode from one window to the next, we talked about many things: the conference, pharmacologists and scientists we had met, historic monuments we had visited for days, and a little about Japanese monuments and Zen gardens. As we walked by Kwality Restaurant, the guard opened the door for us to enter. The aromas of lunch food wafted through the door.

"Hungry, Professor?"

"You too?"

We had lunch at the restaurant where the food was spicy and the prices reasonable. He insisted on paying the bill, but eventually decided to go Dutch. By late afternoon, he had purchased several silk scarves and ties, a woodcarving of Ganesh—the god of beginnings, a bronze statue of Nataraja—the god of cosmic creation and dissolution, a stone image of the seated Buddha, one gold bracelet, and two gold earrings. Satisfied with his purchases, I asked if he would like to visit the Red Fort, a famous Mughal monument. But he said his flight was early the next morning, and he did not want to exhaust himself.

"What about an early, home-cooked dinner?" I asked. He looked pleasantly surprised and thanked me; then I drove him to my home.

It had been a long, hot, and humid day. We were sweating when I knocked at the front door. My mother opened and greeted Mr. Ishadate by joining her palms. I had told her about my new friend—more than she wanted to know. He reciprocated her greeting by bowing several times. She ushered us into the drawing room and asked us to be comfortable and cool ourselves. Then she returned to the kitchen.

We sat on cushioned wooden chairs under a ceiling fan that ran at full speed, our wet shirts drying, our bodies cooling. My mother returned with a tray holding two glasses of freshly squeezed cold lemonade.

"What mother cooking?" Ishadate asked after my mother had returned to the kitchen and as the aroma of roasted red pepper and cumin seeds hit our nostrils.

"Frying spices for some dal. Would you like to watch her?" I said.

"She will mind?"

"No!" I called, "Ma! Can we watch you cook?"

"Kitchen is not clean!"

"He doesn't care about that! He just wants to see how you cook!" I called back.

"Okay, come in," she said.

The kitchen was so small that we stood close behind, flanking her as she rolled out rounds of puri with dough she had kneaded earlier. One puri was deep-frying in hot oil, turning golden and puffing up at the surface.

"Mother of gol gappa! Yah?" he mused. "This how gol gappas made?"

"What is he saying?" my mother asked.

"He says they look like large gol gappas and wants to know if this is how they too are made," I translated.

"Yes, exactly! Only bigger." She strained the puri and gently pressed another puri that was frying in the oil.

I translated what she told me for our guest.

Not wishing to crowd my mother in the hot kitchen, the professor returned to the drawing room, and I followed. How else to entertain him? I wondered, and switched on a twelve-inch black-and-white television set. A news anchor delivered the news, but his image scrolled in quick succession and went kaput. The screen started to snow.

"Purchased it from a friend." I smiled sheepishly as I adjusted the TV antennae. "Secondhand! Does this often." I tapped the top and slapped the sides several times. Usually, that did the trick, and the image stabilized. But this time it didn't work. The professor said jokingly, "Machines tick when you kick. Right?" We both laughed. Somewhat embarrassed, I turned off the television. He must have a new color TV at his home, I thought, and why not? The Japanese manufacture the best televisions in the world.

My mother set the dining table, which had been pushed against the wall between the kitchen and the drawing room. She called us to the table. When Professor Ishadate pulled out a chair for her, she giggled like a schoolgirl and said in Hindi to me, "Tell him I'll eat after making a few more puris. *Garam, garam khao*, eat them warm!"

When I translated what she had said, he hesitated a few moments before sitting on the chair I had pulled out for him. On a steel plate, Ma placed two puris, a serving of aromatic rice with green peas, a bowl of moong dal, and a bowl of cauliflower. I showed him how to use pieces of puri to scoop spoonfuls of dal and morsels of cauliflower florets. He learned quickly and had no use for a spoon and fork. When Ma served more puris, he used them to eat rice.

We talked about good Indian restaurants in Tokyo where he often dined with his wife and children. When their children and grandchildren visited, they made it a point to have a meal at their favorite Indian restaurant. Their children seemed to like the cuisine as much as he and his wife did. Then Ma came in and asked if she could get us anything. Usually she and I ate together, but when I brought a friend for dinner, she did not join us, preferring instead to eat later.

"Mother's food—most tasty. Thank you for your trouble!" he said, looking at her, and then asked me to translate. Before I could do so, my mother said she understood.

Before leaving, the professor again thanked my mother for a delicious meal. She folded her palms in return and thanked him for coming.

I drove him back to the hotel. Before going in, he held my hands in his and said, "Thank you! Thank you for hospitality! Please visit Tokyo someday!" I thanked him for the invitation and went home.

Almost two years passed. One morning, Mr. Mehra called me to his office. He congratulated me for being on the list of Indian delegates invited by the University of Tokyo for that year's International Pharmaceutical Conference. My expenses were paid in full, but Mr. Mehra was puzzled that Professor Ishadate had requested a two-day leave for me after the conference. Did I know this professor? I reminded him that I had been the professor's tour guide when he came to the international conference in New Delhi.

At the Tokyo airport, a man was holding a placard with my name. I introduced myself to him, and he bowed and said his name was Yamamoto. He was going to be my guide during my stay in the city. As we drove toward the hotel where the conference was being held, he did not say who had engaged him or who had arranged my stay. Before dropping me off at my hotel, he said I was to meet Professor Tetsu Ishadate that evening.

Several hours later, Yamamoto came back to pick me up. We drove for a half hour through the heart of Tokyo and stopped in front of a tall building with a sign that read *Ishadate Pharmaceutical Industries.* As we walked through the front gate, I found myself walking into a strikingly different atmosphere—bonsai trees reflecting in miniature waterfalls and ikebana arrangements aesthetically placed on pedestals in front of floor-to-ceiling glass walls.

Riding the elevator with my guide, I nervously looked at my reflection to see if I was presentable. When we exited the elevator, a door came into view that read *Tetsu Ishadate, CEO.* An attendant opened the door to a luxurious office. Yamamoto beckoned me to go in while he waited outside. The attendant closed the door, and I recognized the man seated behind a large table. Ishadate walked toward me with an extended hand.

"How are you, Mohan?" he said. We shook hands and he bowed. He had the same smile and twinkle in his eyes that had charmed me the first time I met him. I noticed our pictures from Jantar Mantar on the shelf behind him.

"Fine, I am fine, Professor! Thanks for your recommendation!" I replied.

"Thank you, you come! Mother, how is she?"

"She is fine and sends her regards," I said as I looked at the beautifully paneled walls. "I thought you were a professor."

"Part-time only. This full time job," he said, tapping on the table.

"TV working?" He smiled.

"I got it fixed," I said sheepishly.

"Sorry, Mohan! I attend important meeting in Osaka." He bowed his head.

"You won't be able to attend the conference then?" I was hoping to spend some time with him.

"Mr. Yamamoto show my office," he said, and instructed Yamamoto to give me a tour of the facility.

My jaw fell as Yamamoto showed me the working robots that Ishadate's company had built to efficiently and safely dispense drugs. The manufacturing facility was a world in itself. The robots were capable of scanning barcodes on medications and ordering, dispensing, and administering drugs. Yamamoto, I learned, was an assistant manager in the company. He said, "Most of the credit goes to the professor and his team for their research and development. They have made it possible to improve communication between nursing and pharmacy, and also increase the safety of dispensing medication from the pharmacy to the patient's bedside."

Seeing my enthusiasm, he took me to all the floors. The tour lasted for an hour; the he drove me back to my hotel.

I spent my conference days attending lectures and workshops and participating in discussions. During the evenings, in the company of a few other delegates I befriended, we tasted Japanese cuisine while networking. My task was to write two articles for my company's bi-monthly magazine. One article was to be about new drugs for AIDS and the second about the new chemotherapy capsules for blood cancer. We ate bento box lunches that included tempura and sushi accompanied by pickled ginger and wasabi paste. I liked it but missed my chutneys and chili-peppered meals.

The morning after the conference ended, Yamamoto drove me to the airport where Professor Ishadate surprised me. We bid good-bye to Yamamoto and took a flight to Kyoto.

From the Kyoto airport, a limousine drove us directly to the Zen temple of Daitoku-ji. The exquisite Daisen-in temple that I had seen in photographs was a pale resemblance of what I was standing in. I had been transported to the most serene surroundings. Following Ishadate as he led me through the outer gardens of Daisen-in, we saw monks wearing straw hats squatting on dewy green moss, clearing fallen yellowed leaves and twigs, leaving the area spotless. A stone pathway led to the inner garden where a stream's gentle sounds greeted us. On a rock in the water, a white-eye bird sat watching a Mandarin duck cleaning its beak.

A stone path led us to a dry landscape. Instead of grass, the whole garden was of stones, gravel, and rocks. Another monk raked circles and waves on the white gravel. The professor explained that his design would remain until the next day when the monk would rake a new design. Seven rocks of various sizes jutted from the gravel. We sat on the steps overlooking the dry garden to contemplate what the monk had composed. The monochromatic dry garden conjured up a feeling of tranquility. The silence and stillness grounded me, helped deepen my attention. I inhaled the air slowly and deeply, trying to take it all in.

We stayed in a nearby hotel that night, and I slept well and woke refreshed, looking forward to another day with my gracious host. After breakfast, we were driven to a teahouse nestled in a forested area. We walked on a long stone pathway that led to a teahouse nestled behind the trees.

Here, at once, our connection with the outside world seemed to break. We rinsed our hands in a hand-carved stone basin and crouched to enter the teahouse. Light filtered through the paper windows reflecting on an ikebana and, behind it, a scroll painting.

Already in the room was the tea master watching puffs of steam escape from the spout of an iron kettle. Ishadate bowed, introduced me to him, then sat with me cross-legged on the tatami floor. The tea master held a ceramic cup in his left hand and put two spoonfuls of emerald green powder in it. He mixed the powder with steaming water by pouring a few spoonfuls of water at a time. He whisked the mixture until it was frothy, then he poured it into two cups and handed them to us. He served us sweet buns on a napkin decorated with a drawing of a cherry blossom.

In silence, we slowly sipped the tea and tasted the buns while the master wiped the utensils he had used to prepare the tea. Then he passed them around for us to admire: the ceramic bowl, the whisk, and the spoon. Our senses of taste, smell, and sight thus stimulated, we appreciated the simplicity and serenity of the exquisite ritual.

That afternoon, we flew from Kyoto to the Tokyo airport, where I was to take my flight home. I thanked the professor for his hospitality and promised to stay in touch. Before departing for the terminal, we embraced.

During my short visit to Japan, I had experienced the two most peaceful days of my life. They had stirred something deep within me, a sense of peace I could not explain but would carry with me for the rest of my life.

I was overwhelmed by the professor's generosity. He had recommended my name for the Tokyo conference, then generously guided me through the

Zen Gardens. What a magnanimous man! When he visited India, I had simply treated him the way I did because I was attracted to his charm and simple manners. As my mother often said, "We should treat our guests the way we receive our gods".

From New Delhi airport, I hired a three-wheeler to my home. My mother greeted me at the door. In the middle of the drawing room, I saw a big cardboard box.

"What is this?" I asked my mother.

"It was delivered yesterday. The man said it is from Japan. I was surprised myself".

It was from the professor. I cut through the tape and pulled out the flaps. Snug between the packing materials was a twenty-two-inch color television.

YELLOW JACKET

I parked my car and dragged my feet towards my apartment. My head throbbed. Holding my bulging briefcase and Chinese takeout, I fumbled with my keys. Finding the key, I opened the door. The telephone was ringing, but I wasn't going to answer it. What if it was Nandi, my fiancé? I thought. Dropping the briefcase on the floor and putting my dinner on the kitchen table, I walked to the telephone.

"Hello!" I said.

"Sir, this is Alka's nephew . . . I don't know how to . . . I'm sorry to have to tell you that . . . that Muni is dead."

"Dead! How? When?" My heart hammered and I slumped on the sofa. The scent of Muni's musk cologne still lingered in my apartment.

#

Ten years ago, when I emigrated to America to pursue a doctoral program in statistics, Muni had just turned fifteen. After finishing college in India with some difficulty, he started an Indian clothing and jewelry business that eventually flourished. While I wrestled with statistics, he exported women's silk and cotton dresses to the United States and Bollywood fashion to Hollywood celebrities. The demand for his clothing was so great that he opened an office in America and settled in Pittsburgh.

Since emigrating to the U.S., I had seen Muni only three times: first, on our mother's birthday when I happened to be in India; second, last May at his wedding—again in India; and finally when he and his wife, Alka, came to visit me yesterday. When they arrived several hours late, I greeted them at the door. Dressed colorfully in yellows and pinks, they looked out of place in my stark apartment. The only spot of color in the room was the bunch of flowers Nandi had brought the previous evening.

Nine years my junior, Muni was dressed like a peacock and smelled of musk. Seeing him in a yellow cashmere jacket, I bitterly thought how good things always seemed to fall at his feet.

"We're sorry for being late!" Alka had said. I smelled her jasmine perfume. "Meow got lost. It took hours before the maid found her."

"Where did she go?" I asked.

"Nowhere too far! We finally found her in our back woods, huddled under a mulberry bush. We didn't want to leave until she was home safe. You understand."

"Sorry, Bhaiya!" Muni said, using an affectionate term for his older brother. "A few friends dropped in last evening. This morning, they asked if they could splash in the pool—I couldn't say no! Sorry, we lost track of time."

A pool! I tried to push down the rising envy in my belly. "Isn't it a pain to maintain a pool?"

"Not if someone else is doing it for you," Muni replied, casually making himself comfortable on the sofa. Alka sat next to him.

"Someone else? Like who?" I asked.

"We have a pool cleaning service," Alka said.

I ordered dinner on the phone and busied myself setting the table with paper plates, cups, and plastic forks. Muni got up from his chair. "Oops!" he said, thumping his head. "I'll be back!" And he hurried out the door.

"Bhaiya," Alka said, gently turning to where I was standing, "another reason we were late was because Muni went to three stores in search of your favorite beer. At first, he even hesitated to bring it."

"Why?"

"Out of respect. You know he thinks of you like a father. You're the only father he has known."

I was surprised to hear she thought of me as Muni's father, something I did not feel. I had my grudges against our father and mother and felt envious of Muni having been spared some of those feelings. Alka continued to talk candidly about her loving-giving-considerate Muni.

Such a Muni I did not know.

Muni returned with a six-pack of my favorite Indian beer and a bottle of red wine for Alka.

The conversation turned to their honeymoon in Hawaii. "You've got to go to Hawaii!" Alka said, sipping her wine.

This rich, spoiled couple had no idea of my financial conditions. They told stories about their blissful time together.

"And then the honeymoon was over, literally!" Muni said, swirling the wine in his glass, and they both laughed. "After we returned, we hired a contractor to build our dream house. What a pain in the butt that was! It cost us triple the estimate he gave us.

"We wouldn't be living in that house if her parents had not bailed us out," Muni said, squeezing her shoulder.

After dinner, they held hands and asked why Nandi and I didn't visit them and why I had not invited her that evening. I made some excuse and said it was eleven and I was tired. I would sleep on the sofa and asked them to make themselves comfortable in my bedroom. At first, they hesitated, but when I insisted, they yielded.

After breakfast, Alka took some pictures of Muni and me together, then they left. When I went to get my coat from the closet, Muni's yellow cashmere jacket was hanging there. Glancing at it, for some reason I put it on and looked at myself in the mirror. I looked like a pimp, I thought. How is a man expected to look decent in yellow!

I taught introductory courses in statistics, tutored school children, and on the weekends, worked on my research. The rest of my time was taken up running errands and doing household chores. My life was a colorless routine with little zest, and I no longer felt passion for my chosen field. The only stroke of color in my gray days was Nandi. Yet, at times, I wondered why I had even gotten engaged.

Last week, on my hand-me-down sofa, she cuddled beside me. And what did I do? Whine to her about my work, my boring life, my inability to finish my doctorate, thus not having a decent enough job to get married.

"You need a change," she suggested. "A short break, new scenery, something, anything away from your routine . . . I know underneath that sheath you are hiding an exciting man with a heart of gold. A break would do wonders."

"You always say that! And where will the money come from, *han*?" I retorted.

"Everything doesn't have to do with money! I'm going to tell you something that I have never said before—you are the one responsible for your boring, colorless life! We have enough to get married. Together, we make enough to move to a better apartment," she said, nervously arranging the bouquet of flowers she brought. "Your problem is you focus more on what you don't have than on what you do!"

"No, I don't!" I said with false conviction. In my heart of hearts, I knew she was right. Yet I quickly dismissed her.

#

On one of our mother's birthdays, I happened to be in India. Muni had gone missing the whole day, and in the evening, Ma sent the servant to look for him. The servant searched for Muni at his usual hangouts, but the boy was nowhere to be found. She was in no mood to celebrate, open her gifts, or eat dinner. Restlessly, we waited for Muni to come home. Ma became more frantic by the minute.

Finally, when Muni appeared, he was hiding something behind his back. His smiling face made me angrier, but our mother looked greatly relieved and didn't utter a single angry word or reprimand. What a spoiled brat! I thought.

Pretending to be stern, she said, "Where were you? You worried me to death! We were about to call . . ." Before she could finish her thought, he extended his hand, which held a wrapped gift.

"Happy birthday, Ma!" he said, placing the package in front of her.

Her firmness melted into a smile and a joyous hug. She unwrapped the gift; it was a bottle of her favorite perfume.

"Where on earth did you get the money to buy this?" she asked.

"How did you manage to buy such an expensive gift?" I asked. The fact that I had forgotten Ma's birthday did not diminish my unease or envy.

"The tiffin wallah went to his sister's wedding in his village, so I offered to take his route."

"Oh, my son! Is that true? What would neighbors say?" Ma said.

"Working like a servant. What's wrong with you?" I chided, taking advantage of my status as an elder brother.

Our mother wiped her eyes with the end of her sari, and I was too green-eyed to say anything further. My lips were sealed, lest I make a fool of myself.

#

And now Muni was dead! My throat felt dry and my limbs weak, even though I was sitting on the sofa. Still I managed to stand up and get myself a drink of water.

Calling my brother's house, I learned that Muni had been speeding on his red Harley-Davidson when it skidded and turned full circle on wet road, throwing him over a bridge. He plunged onto the railway track below. He wasn't wearing a helmet, and his skull was smashed. He was brought by ambulance to the hospital and died in the emergency room.

My heart felt stuck in my throat, and I thought of my mother in India. I didn't have the heart to call her just then. Instead, I went to Muni's home.

#

Walking past dozens of cars parked on the street, I approached the front door of the mansion. Cries and lamentations filtered through the front door. Instead of ringing the doorbell, I pushed the door open and entered on unsteady legs. I did not recognize any of the mourners, and no one seemed to know me either. Some watched, some whispered.

I sat on a corner chair and searched for a familiar face. Alka's mother, a dignified woman, what Alka might look like twenty-five years hence, sat next to me. She comforted me as I tried to console her. She told me about the accident, and Alka's father soon joined us. I asked if I could be of any use, if I could help them in any way. The father said I was in mourning and not to worry about anything. Everything was taken care of. The funeral arrangements were made. They were waiting for the police to release the body. My little brother had turned into a body! My earlier feeling of jealousy transformed into enormous guilt. No longer was I envious, but how was I to get rid of this guilt? Was Muni really dead? Couldn't he come to life momentarily to relieve me of the emotional load that would sink me into oblivion? At that moment, I heard Alka scream.

Alka's mother said that Alka had fainted when she heard about the accident. When she came to her senses, she was unsure of who or where she was. "Unaware of her surroundings," Alka's mother sobbed. "A bride of eleven months already widowed!" I did my best to console Alka and her mother, and her father asked me to stay with them until the day of the funeral.

The next day, I watched Alka move about in a daze. She refused to believe Muni was dead. She cooked tandoori chicken for dinner and waited for him to come home. She stayed up until she could not keep her eyes open. The day Muni's body was released, she prepared mushroom-stuffed manicotti, his favorite.

As I sat amongst the mourners, a memory was triggered of the day Muni was born. My grandmother brought me to the hospital because by then our father had left us. I gazed at my mother lying on the hospital bed breastfeeding Muni as she gently stroked his forehead with her thumb. My grandmother sighed saying 'premature' and 'anemic' but Ma shushed her.

"This is your little brother," Ma whispered without looking at me, her face pale, her voice weak. I wanted her to stroke my head. To pick me up and hold me in her lap the way she was holding the baby. The way she had before her love had shifted to this thing at her bosom. For days after mother and son returned home, I was not kissed or patted or stroked. She was constantly preoccupied with little Muni, and those days were like years to me. The tinges of jealousy for the one who had snatched my mother away grew into an emotional wound, and I never fully understood its significance. My mother's neglect had created an emotional gap between Muni and me. Through the years, the wound festered until it undermined my relationship with him. And mind you, it was one-sided—it was my wound, my pain. But now, it was too late for regret. Too late.

#

At the funeral home, Alka sat with stooped shoulders in the front row, flanked by her parents. I sat behind them. After fifteen minutes or so, Alka stood up, walked to the casket, and stared at the body. I stood next to her. Muni's body lay in an open casket, his head carefully reconstructed. I recognized him from the pudgy hands that had been placed one over the other. As she was about to touch Muni's face, the funeral director came running.

"Please," he pleaded, "please, madam, do not touch it."

Alka called to her mother, "Mom, why won't this man let me touch Muni?" Then, turning toward the director, she said, "Why? Why shouldn't I touch him? Isn't he my husband? Why doesn't he talk to me? Why? Tell me! Why?"

Alka's mother came running. The director and I stood in silence as her mother held Alka close around her waist.

Alka turned to the body and said, "Wake up, M, please wake up! This is no time for your practical jokes." Then she turned to the director. "He doesn't look like my husband. Are you sure it is him? Bhaiya, you tell me, does this person look like Muni to you?"

I stood motionless, staring helplessly at Muni's reconstructed head and face.

I was one of four men who carried Muni's casket to the crematorium on the ground floor of the funeral. Alka followed with her parents tightly holding each of her arms. We piled sandalwood logs on the casket. Because Muni did not have a son, I lit the burners, a painful responsibility of the last rite. The logs blazed, and the roar of the flames jolted Alka from her daze.

"I'm suffocating," she cried. "I'm burning!" She screamed so loudly that her wail pierced the hearts of those present. Then she fell unconscious.

When I felt strong enough to call our frail mother, she told me someone from Alka's family had already called. Since then, she had not spoken a word. She had hummed lullabies until her throat was dry and lamented until there were no more tears.

I accompanied Alka when she carried Muni's ashes to India. They were immersed at the confluence of the Yamuna and Ganges Rivers. A few days later, I bade farewell to my mother.

#

Back home in my apartment, guilt gnawed at me. I looked around at the bare windows and shelves stacked with one dull book after another. One night, a month after the immersion of Muni's ashes, I awoke in the middle of the night, sweating. If only, if only I had been a good brother! The words continued to circle my mind.

I wrote a letter to Muni saying that he was worthy of my love and appreciation, but I had offered nothing. I was a rotten older brother; envious of him from the day he was born—of his looks, his luck, his charm. I was selfish. I was blind to his goodness. I asked for his forgiveness. Then I read what I had written, and then reread it several times. What was the use of this sham repentance? Where had I been when Muni was alive? Would the pain ever cease? What was the use of this letter? I thought, and tore it to pieces.

#

Five months later, I passed my doctoral exams and got a job. I started to visit Alka. Her delirium had disappeared. With the help of her family and friends, she slowly regained her emotional strength and seemed to appreciate my regular visits.

One Saturday afternoon, I took Nandi to meet Alka and brought the yellow cashmere jacket with me.

"This is Nandi," I said as she greeted us at the door. Alka seemed to have put on weight.

"She's pretty!" Alka said, and gave Nandi a hug.

We sat by the pool drinking fresh lemonade.

"Alka, I finally remembered to bring it," I said, pointing to the yellow jacket.

She rubbed the jacket against her cheek and then pointed to a photograph on the table. "He is wearing it in this picture." It was the picture of Muni and me she had taken the day they visited my apartment.

As I looked at it, the picture began to blur.

"Take that picture!" she said. "And please, keep the jacket. He would have liked you to have something of his." The yellow color looked comforting, and I held the jacket in my lap.

Alka talked at length about how much she missed Muni. I shared several stories of the good times Muni and I had had. She listened attentively. Soon, it was time for us to leave. At the door, Alka said, "Don't forget to invite us to the wedding."

"Us?" Nandi asked.

Her black eyes brightened. "Bhaiya, soon, you're going to be an uncle!"

#

The following month, Nandi and I moved to a new apartment. We purchased a Kashmiri carpet, a set of curtains the color of sunshine, and a new sofa and mattress. I bought a handsome frame for Muni's picture, which we hung on the wall between the two windows. Muni will feel at home here, I thought. For the first time, since long ago in childhood, I too felt at home.

DARKNESS BEHIND EYES

Lyn watched with envy as Vanessa, her neighbor across the street, collected her mail. Almost every day, just before lunchtime, Lyn looked out the kitchen window and saw Vanessa glide out her front door. Today Vanessa was holding who knows how many pieces of mail. She waved to Lyn and walked back inside.

Someone somewhere had a lot to say to Vanessa, and she to them. How fortunate she was to be literate and able to communicate. Lyn wondered what people wrote about— their daily troubles and joys, their loving families, their work experience, the exotic places they visited? She breathed deeply trying to rid herself of her pangs of jealousy, but the feelings of envy refused to leave her.

At seventy-two, Lyn lived alone in the same Pennsylvania farmhouse in which she had been born. But, one by one, family members either moved away or passed on. No other families lived within miles of Lyn, except for Vanessa, her spinster neighbor.

Lyn could neither read nor write, though she had always wanted to. Family circumstances had kept her from going to school. After her mother's death, ten-year-old Lyn was the only female in the house, so she took over the responsibility of caring for her younger siblings. She spent her teenage years doing household chores and looking after two younger brothers. When she was in her twenties her father was diagnosed with Alzheimer's disease, and things fell apart. Until then, he had helped manage the household. He had been the assistant manager of the grocery store in town, but memory lapses and absentmindedness made it impossible to continue working. At first when he stayed home he was able to help Lyn with household chores. Then, in time, a thick cloud of vagueness enveloped him. Lyn functioned as his mind, and the last four years of his life were devastating. In caring for her father, Lyn forgot to care for herself.

Twenty-four hours a day, Lyn tended to her father's physical needs. During the period he needed constant care, Lyn's brothers, Donavan and David, were already gone from the family home, one to college and the other to the West Coast. They still came home once or twice a year, and not necessarily for Thanksgiving or Christmas, but at their convenience. Before long, their visits dwindled to once a year. Lyn continued to care for her father, and when he finally died, she was almost forty.

Lyn wasn't bitter nor lonely; watching her mother and father suffer and die and witnessing the fleeting nature of life had mellowed her. Experience had taught her to focus on what was at hand and find solace in a solitary existence. Having lived most of her young adult life taking care of the people she loved, she had matured and grown to appreciate solitude. Her only regret was never having learned to read and write.

But today, as Lyn watched Vanessa gather her mail, it did not bother her so much. Her favorite niece, Meredith, would be coming to spend the summer and autumn with her! Lyn had come to depend on Meredith's help, for she took care of Lyn's paperwork—the mortgage, utility bills, banking—anything that required one to read and write. Lyn not only loved her niece but also felt obligated to her.

Meredith planned to write her first book in Aunt Lyn's farmhouse. "Your home is one of the most inspiring and peaceful places, Aunt!" she had said on the telephone. The news of her visit gladdened Lyn. Meredith was in her mid-thirties and had been a journalist of repute. But she had quit her job because she wanted to travel and teach English. Two years ago, her dream had come true, and she was now teaching children in remote villages worldwide.

When Meredith took flights to reach her destinations, Lyn prayed for her safe journey and healthy stay at those unknown places with unfamiliar names: Myanmar, Bhutan, Taiwan, Guatemala. The only name she recognized was India. After her return, Meredith entertained her with fascinating stories about the children she taught. She was going to write a book about her teaching experiences in the various countries.

When the day came for her to be there, Lyn couldn't think of anything else but *Meredith is coming! Meredith is coming!* Lyn paced from the bedroom window to the kitchen. Every ten minutes or so, she peered through the kitchen curtains looking for Meredith's car on the distant road. The wind through the windows blew her gray hair like a halo around her wrinkled face. While she waited, she imagined Meredith in a Taiwanese village teaching under the shade of a tree, then in a Guatemalan open-air classroom and a brick school in Myanmar. Recently, Meredith had been teaching English to a class of Indian girls with oiled and tightly braided hair and she imagined them with smiles on their lips and hope in their eyes. She thought about Meredith in sneakers on dusty unpaved paths and dirt roads. She recalled her thick blond hair and freckled face. She imagined her niece teaching students, "her girls," as Meredith called them, neatly copying what was written in white chalk on the blackboard. She imagined the students repeating the words Meredith had written on the board. Imagining Meredith at in the classroom made Lyn giddy with pride.

Across the street, Lyn spotted Vanessa. This time, she did not glide back into her house but turned around, looked up, and gave Lyn a smile. Lyn smiled back and sighed, thinking how nice it would be to get heartwarming letters.

"Hey, Vanessa!" cried Lyn excitedly. "My niece is coming to stay with me for the summer."

"How nice!" Vanessa said, then walked back into her house and closed the door behind her. Vanessa's indifference did not register in Lyn's mind; she was too preoccupied with anticipating her niece's arrival.

Lyn blinked. Several decades ago, when Meredith was ten, Lyn had wanted to drive away, simply get in a car and drive until she reached the end of the world. At a rare holiday gathering, an uncle from her father's side of the family had asked Lyn that if she could be granted any wish, what would it be? At first she did not want to say. She felt as if her life had been directed by fate so desiring something was pointless. But something made her say she wished she could be a teacher of children in exotic lands. Everyone at the holiday party looked at her as if she had lost her mind—except Meredith, who took her hand and gazed admiringly at her, and said, "Why don't you, then?" Her words, innocent yet wise, had amused the company but also made Lyn think. She had never tried to take control of her life. Destiny may have a role to play, but she was free to choose her path.

When Meredith made the remark, she didn't know that Aunt Lyn didn't even know the alphabet. But now Meredith was coming from the world out there. She had seen, smelled, heard, tasted, and touched it. And she was going to write a book about it. She would tell her aunt about the world out there as if she too were one of "her girls."

Lyn saw the sun glinting on a car coming towards the house. She ran down the steps, out the front door, and down the path as Meredith drove in and parked.

"Meredith!" Lyn said hugging her tightly. "Welcome!"

Meredith hugged her back. Then she held Lyn's face between her palms and kissed both of her cheeks. "How are you, Aunt Lyn?"

Lyn's eyes welled with tears. She could not say a word. Her voice choked in her throat.

"Why are you crying?" Meredith asked.

Lyn gently removed her niece's hands from her face and linked her fingers through hers to make sure she was not dreaming. "Because you're here!" she said, giddy with happiness. "You are here!"

Lyn stood still in the presence of this adventurer, this teacher, this beautiful blond who had travelled to remote villages to shine the light of literacy. It was a different world from that of Lyn's. She felt too in awe of Meredith to move.

"Are we going in or what?" Meredith had taken her suitcase out of the trunk.

"We are! We are!" Lyn said and led her inside.

#

A week passed. Meredith settled comfortably into the bedroom next to Lyn's, opposite the kitchen. The atmosphere was languid, and felt as if she had lived at the farmhouse forever.

One morning, just like every other, the aroma of fresh coffee awoke Meredith. The previous night had been productive. Instead of getting under the sheets to sleep, she had propped herself against the pillows on her bed and written until her wrist hurt. Sunrays were filtering through the window when she woke. She got out of bed, pulled apart the white muslin curtains, flung open the window, and let the mountain breeze flow in. The air was fragrant with pine; the birds stirred on the branches of the majestic oaks outside her bedroom. How she loved listening to the buzzing of insects, looking at the buttercups and myrtles blooming, watching honeybees collect pollen, and grasshoppers fling themselves on the grass. The ideas from the night's writing still circled in her mind.

"I have a big breakfast ready for you!" Lyn called from the kitchen.

"What are you going to spoil me with today?" Meredith called back.

"Well, today, my darling, you will eat poached eggs, my homemade bread, bacon, and your Indian cocktail—sugary coffee with milk. And I also have your favorite blueberry preserves."

Meredith came to the kitchen table with her yellow notebook intending to jot down ideas after eating. Lyn had laid the table with a sumptuous breakfast. Finally, she sat facing Meredith and said, "Eat! I know you worked until the late hours last night. You must be famished."

"That I am!" Meredith said and sipped her coffee and bit into a slice of bacon. "Yummyyyyyyy! To die for! I could have this every day, any time of the day!" she said, helping herself to toast with preserves. Suddenly, she was quiet, thinking as she pressed the pencil with her index finger and moved it to and fro. Then she scribbled something with her long yellow pencil.

In a breathless spell, Lyn watched her write and then lazily rest the pencil on the notebook. She had never held a pencil or a pen. Her hand twitched on the handle of her coffee cup as she took a sip.

"How does it feel to write?" Lyn asked.

"Hmmm?"

"I said how does it feel to write?" Meredith looked at Lyn and made marks on the pad.

"I will tell you how it feels, but first tell me: What does this say?" Meredith pointed to the words she had just made.

"You know, darling, I can't read."

"I know, that's why I'm asking you to look at these letters. . ." Meredith said, pointing to each letter one by one, "Look at this. This is an L and Y and N. That makes Lyn."

"My name!" Lyn grinned widely and excitedly. She pushed a slice of bread with a layer of blueberry preserves towards her niece. "Eat!" she commanded.

"Thanks!" Meredith took a bite, chewed, gulped it down with coffee, and said, "Do you want to write something?" She pulled out a new pencil and a small notebook from her bag.

Lyn smiled. "No, I don't think so. It's fun watching you write though . . . although . . . I would love to write a letter . . . get a reply . . . but I don't know a soul . . . who would write to me?"

"You can't expect a letter unless you write one, can you?"

Lyn looked at the pencil in Meredith's hand and held her breath.

"Come on, let's write something!" Meredith extended her hand, holding a pad and a pencil.

Hesitantly, Lyn took it. She placed the pad on the table, held the pencil in her hand, and gazed at the pad. She turned to Meredith.

"Go ahead, try!" She looked thoughtfully for a few moments at her aunt. "There is darkness behind your eyes, Aunt," Meredith said. "But learning letters and words will make you see with a different light."

Lyn squinted, licked the sharpened head of the pencil, and set it on the paper. She breathed deep, gathering courage to start a new venture. At that moment, she saw movement through the kitchen window. Vanessa floated out of her front door like a flower on a rippling river.

"I need to mail a few letters. What time does the postman come?" Meredith asked.

"I don't know, darling, said Lyn. " Come to think of it, I don't even know who the postman is. But Vanessa would know. She gets mail every day."

After breakfast was over, Meredith went back to writing and Lyn to cleaning up and preparing for lunch. Every time she passed Meredith's room, the sound of paper shuffling and pencil scribbling animated her like nothing else.

Summer days turned into weeks and weeks into a month. The days when she had time on her hands, she walked into Meredith's room and stood behind her. Lyn considered the quick smile her niece gave her as permission to watch her write. In wonderment, she observed how she made curves, dots, and lines. That these shapes had meaning was like magic to her. On one such occasion, as Lyn lovingly gazed at Meredith's right hand, she tilted her head and said, "Sorry to interrupt you, darling, but it amuses me to think that sometimes I feel I recognize your hand better than your face. I know every part of your hand, every bump and crinkle, making squiggles and doodles."

"You look amazed," Meredith said, resting her long yellow pencil on the paper.

"Read me something," Lyn said, sitting on the edge of the bed facing Meredith's writing table.

Meredith thought for a moment, took a book from her bag, flipped through a few pages, and began to read aloud. "What sets us above all other creatures on this planet is our ability to read and write. What we thus understand determines our relationship with the world."

Rapt and wide-eyed, Lyn said, "Read me some more!"

Meredith flipped through a few pages, scanned one, and flipped some more. Then she read.

"Listen, Aunt." She cleared her throat. "When you teach a man to read and write, you educate an individual; when you teach a woman to read and write, you educate a family—nay, an entire community."

With her eyes fixed on the floor Lyn pondered. *How different would her world be? What new things would she really see if she too could read and write?* She did not know that a literate woman could benefit her community more than a literate man! What other hundreds of things did she not know that a person who could read and write might know? Meredith had said that each one of us has the ability to learn anything we wanted if we put our mind to it. Thinking of this, Lyn said, "Darling, write what I say."

With pencil in hand, Meredith smiled, nodded, and waited.

"Write 'Meredith loves Aunt Lyn . . . Meredith will teach Lyn how to read and write letters.'"

Meredith wrote down what Lyn had said. When she looked up, Lyn's face was somber. "What's wrong, Aunt Lyn?"

"Nothing," Lyn said. Then she quickly added, "No. There is something. I am thinking about the whole process of wanting to say something, then putting it in curves, lines, and dots on paper, and sending it to someone thousands of miles away who will understand what this scribbling means. And then write back to me. I will be able to read. I will not only read letters but also magazines, newspapers, books, anything I want. This is amazing, simply amazing . . ."

"I guess it is," Meredith said casually, squinting at the pad.

"No, no, it certainly is! It is as amazing as the day you were born—almost miraculous!"

"Human birth is a miracle, but this is not a miracle," Meredith said, tapping the sheet she had just written on.

"It certainly is! You have the power to articulate what is in your mind by the mere movement of a yellow pencil," Lyn said. Her cheeks flushed.

"You can learn, too."

"At my age?"

"At any age! Do you want to start right now?"

"Are you serious? Can I?"

"It depends on how much you want to."

"You can't even know how much I want to, darling! I didn't think it was possible!" Lyn said with excitement in her eyes.

"Wait a minute." Lyn got up and went to her room. When she returned, she was carrying a tablet and a brand new sharpened yellow pencil.

"Who gave you those?"

"I bought them for myself. In my gut, I somehow knew I would need them someday, that someone would teach me how to write. I didn't know who, when, or how. I simply believed."

Meredith carefully scribed L-Y-N W-I-S-S-E on her notebook, making the sound of each letter as she wrote. Lyn, facing her, slowly copied the letters Meredith had made. She wrote them over and over again until she memorized how to write her full name, LYN WISSE. When she felt ready, she said, "Now." She opened the first page of her tablet and slowly wrote her name, saying aloud each letter as she wrote it. Meredith nodded as she watched. "Great beginning, Aunt!" Meredith exclaimed when Lyn was done.

After that morning, Meredith tutored her aunt daily, and Lyn spent hours practicing the letters and words. The teacher would write a word, pronounce it aloud, and then ask her student to repeat it. Lyn would copy the words. Thus, together, they constructed sentence after sentence, paragraph after paragraph, and read them aloud. Lyn read, copied, and memorized several paragraphs every day. Her progress was speedy. She didn't miss a day of reading, writing, and memorizing. During the first month, she worked only after lunch, but later, she added after-dinner hours to practice what she had learned that morning and afternoon. In short, when she was not cooking, cleaning, or going to the market, she was becoming literate.

Lyn worked so diligently that in four months she was at the middle school level of language comprehension. She read stories to Meredith, first slowly, broken sentence by broken sentence. Gradually, her reading improved. When she made mistakes, Meredith corrected her, never uttering a word of discouragement. And when she did well, Meredith would say how proud she was of her, that she was her chief girl.

"Don't give me that title! I am simply doing what I should have done long ago when I was a girl," Lyn said.

"Believe me, Aunt, you're one of a kind! Your resolve and determination are exemplary!" Such encouraging remarks strengthened Lyn's confidence.

Soon, it was time for Meredith to leave.

"I couldn't have completed my manuscript if I had stayed back in my New York apartment—so distracting," Meredith said as she hugged Lyn goodbye. "And thank you so much, Aunt, for taking care of and spoiling me! We had fun, didn't we?" She held her aunt tightly in her arms. The thought of separation made Lyn's eyes tear up.

"Don't cry! You should be so pleased with your work," Meredith said. She kissed Lyn's cheeks. "I'm so proud of you." She put her arm around Lyn's shoulders.

"The house will feel empty now," Lyn said.

"You won't have time to miss me! You're going to keep very busy with the books and audiotapes and instructional material I will mail you when I get home. You are one of my prized students. Besides, I'll return next summer, like it or not!"

"Love you, darling!" Lyn smiled as she wiped her eyes. "Already looking forward to your next visit."

"Love you back!" Meredith said, and gave her aunt an ivory paperknife as a parting gift.

The books and tapes Meredith mailed helped Lyn make up words and roll them on her tongue just like Meredith had rolled out words on paper. She held her pencil with a strong grip; the way Meredith had held a pencil between her delicate fingers as she wrote each vowel and consonant.

Without missing a day, Lyn listened to the instructional tapes and practiced the lessons she had learned from Meredith. Together, they helped her progress through the levels of reading and writing.

One morning, Lyn sat at her study desk, looking through the front window. She was practicing her lesson when her attention was diverted by a shadow moving at the corner of her eye. It was Vanessa getting her mail. Lyn too could get mail if she wrote a letter. What was she waiting for? But to whom would she write?

Mustering her courage, Lyn set out to write a letter to Meredith. She sat on the chair and pulled it close to the table. She began carefully composing a thank-you note. She took out her new sky blue stationery pad with a red border. On the upper right corner, she wrote LW with a blue pen. Then, lower down on the left side, she began, 'My darling Meredith.' Then, slowly and steadily, she wrote one word and then the next and the next. Each sentence she formed sparked a sense of pride. 'Thank you for teaching me how to read and write. You have always been my favorite niece and now my teacher.' When she finished writing, she looked at her handiwork. It felt like an award to herself. She signed her name, took another good look at the completed letter, folded it firmly, and put it in a matching blue envelope. She neatly addressed it. A sigh of satisfaction escaped her. With a feeling of euphoria, she walked to the local post office, bought a stamp, put it on the envelope, and mailed it. Back home, she eagerly waited for a reply.

After a few days, she began watching for the mailman from the window that overlooked the silver ribbon of road that meandered through the low hills. A week passed. One pleasant afternoon, up the blue hills and through the tall green pines, she heard the sound of the mailman's truck. It finally reached the bend and came to a stop on the dusty road.

Lyn ran out of the door and greeted the mailman seated in his truck. He leaned out the window and said, "Ms. Lyn Wisse?"

"Yes, I am Lyn Wisse!" she cried.

"Mail for you, ma'am. I need a signature." He stepped out of his truck and held a large packet toward her. She signed her name on the line he pointed to, and he gave her the packet.

The truck drove away in a cloud of dust, down the driveway and onto the silver ribbon of road.

'Lyn Wisse' she read aloud on the front of the packet as she walked back to the house. When she reached her writing table, she sat down and carefully opened the parcel with the ivory paperknife. Lyn read the letter aloud to herself, savoring each word—her eyes half-shut and her mouth moving as she spoke each word aloud.

My sweet, sweet Aunt Lyn, it said, *this is the reply to the first letter you ever wrote in your life! (I have enclosed your first letter to me!) How exciting is that? Also historic! Perhaps you would like to frame it along with the reply. So I'll keep it short . . . I have also made arrangements for you with a correspondence school for advanced instructions in reading and writing.*

Lyn read Meredith's letter again and again, savoring its contents until she had almost memorized it. The letter was like bright sunshine on a cold, snowy day. She placed her own letter and Meredith's reply in a box with the locket from her mother and a silver dollar from her father.

She read the other papers in the packet, including an official letter addressed to her.

Dear Ms. Wisse,

Enclosed in this packet are full particulars on how you can complete our six-month course through the mail and earn a certificate in writing competence via the International Correspondence School.

As Lyn worked to complete the course, she kept up a regular correspondence with Meredith, who was working on a two-year project in a village in South India. Eventually she began receiving letters not only from her niece but also from "her girls." Numerous letters from girls in Chennai arrived in Pennsylvania describing a place Lyn had never seen. Dearest Aunt Lyn . . . Dear Ms. Wisse . . . Dear Lyn . . .

One girl wrote: *We love Meredith Teacherji so much that we would love to have you, her favorite auntie, spend winter in our village.*

Letters kept coming and Lyn was very busy. Her mailbox was never empty anymore. She replied to every letter she received. She read and she wrote and replied and wrote some more. On a particularly busy day of writing, she had to soak her sore hand in Epsom salts.

Writing and reading letters had become a morning routine for Lyn. It was the best time of the day, pleasurable and productive. She felt she wanted to share her pleasure with someone other than the girls she had been corresponding with. For months, Vanessa had simply waved at her either at her study's curtained window or when Lyn collected her mail. But recently, she had not even noticed her floating out her front door to the mailbox. Vanessa seemed to stay inside all the time. Lyn felt guilty for being so unfriendly. Was Vanessa not doing well? Should she call her? After all, she was the one who had inspired Lyn to learn to read and write in the first place.

Lyn composed a letter in her mind. Writing down a thought, erasing it, writing a new one, revising it again and again until she knew what she was going to write. Then she wrote:

Dear Vanessa,

It feels funny writing a letter to you when you live just across the street. But you will know why I'm doing this when you read the letter. For so many years, I watched you walk to your mailbox. How I envied you as you pulled out a letter or two! When you mentioned the contents of those letters from your loving cousin Bill or childhood friend Sarah or devoted nephew Timothy, I envied you so much!

But I am happy to say that I was able to transform my envy into learning. My niece Meredith, God bless her, made me realize that learning to read and write was not a gift, but a skill. One could acquire this skill at any age. When I understood that, I went ahead with total dedication. Now my dream has become a reality. I can write letters and receive them. Thanks to you!

I felt guilty for envying you, but I believe writing this thank-you letter will redeem me of my guilt. Please forgive me. I thank you from the bottom of my heart for inspiring me.

With best wishes,
Lyn

Lyn dropped the letter in Vanessa's mailbox. The following afternoon, she went to the market to mail Meredith a bottle of her favorite blueberry preserves. As Lyn walked into the post office, there was Vanessa talking to Jack, the man behind the counter. Lyn walked towards a bench to wait her turn. As she passed Vanessa, she heard Jack read, "I felt guilty for envying you . . . I thank you from the bottom of my heart . . ." He finished and raised his head. When he saw Lyn, he said, "There she is!"

"There who is?" Vanessa turned, and seeing Lyn, raised her eyebrows.

Waving the letter at Lyn, she said, "Now, why on earth would you write me a letter? Couldn't you tell me what you had to say?"

"Was Jack reading my letter to you?" Lyn said. "Why? It was only for you. Why did you show my letter to him?"

"First tell me why you, who lives across the street, would mail me a letter?" Vanessa crossed her arms and straightened her posture.

"Why? Because I wanted to surprise you. To thank you through the written word for inspiring me to fulfill my life's dream."

"How do you mean?" Vanessa's head tilted, her arms fell to her side, and her posture relaxed.

"I watched you receiving mail every day . . ."

"Oh, please, you wretched woman!" Vanessa interrupted. "Don't make me feel worse than I already feel." She turned suddenly and briskly walked out.

Before Lyn could finish saying, "What did I do?" Vanessa was gone.

"What did I do?" Lyn said, turning to Jack.

"Why would you write a letter to someone who doesn't know how to read?" John asked.

"Can't read!" Lyn's jaw dropped.

"Yes!" Jack replied.

Lyn left the building and tried catching up with Vanessa but was unable to cross the road for the speeding traffic. Then Vanessa turned the corner and was out of sight.

Once back at her study, Lyn had an epiphany: Why not teach Vanessa to read and write the way Meredith had taught her? After all, doesn't educating one woman open up possibilities for many more to learn? She collected her introductory books and tapes, a new notebook and a sharpened pencil, and walked toward Vanessa's home.

PORTABLE SHRINE

Last September, I discovered a website called National Novel Writing Month, NaNoWriMo. I was intrigued by the idea of writing a novel in thirty days. I had written a couple of short stories and several website postings in a month, but never a novel. Upon further reading, I learned that the only thing necessary at first was having an idea that had the possibility of growing into a novel. Just sign up, commit to writing a minimum of one thousand, six hundred, sixty-six words each day or night in November—the hours when you did your best work or worst writing didn't matter—and by the end of the month, you would have a sixty-thousand-word first draft that qualified not as a novelette or a novella, but a full-fledged novel.

The idea excited me, and I signed up. As October drew to an end, I was ripe with anticipation and a two-page, single-spaced outline I'd written. I imagined myself in my study longer than usual and not leaving until I had written those one thousand, six hundred, sixty-six words. Yes, I could do it!

My husband is my first reader. He reads the first draft, the revisions, and the final manuscript of everything I write. I did not tell him about my decision to participate in a month of vigorous writing that would result in my first novel. I wanted to surprise him on Nov. 1 by handing him my first day's work, and then every day from then onward.

But something else exciting was happening to us in November. We were expecting our second grandchild, and I worried I might not be able to write my daily word count. Yet that didn't deter my resolve or diminish my enthusiasm. I prepared for the big kick-off, my whole body warm with the anticipation of writing in the solitude and silence of my study.

"This is for you!" My husband handed me an envelope. It was October 24.

"What is this?"

"Open it!"

What I pulled from the envelope was two plane tickets to Cancun. Our flights were booked for October 30. The literary unborn within me kicked hard.

Next week? When and where would I write? Instead of giving him a hug of thanks, I was tongue-tied. I looked at him with questioning eyes. This is what happens when you don't share something with a person with whom you share everything.

"What? Is this the way you thank someone?" he complained.

"I was planning to write every day in November. How can I now? You know I must write in my study. I cannot focus anywhere else. I love to travel, but not as much as I love writing. Egypt and Greece and Italy were great. But I can't go to Mexico, not in November. "

I put the tickets back into the envelope and handed it to him.

He was not angry, but simply said, "You should be able to write anywhere if you put your mind to it."

He knew how deeply I steeped myself in new experiences: monuments and museums, restaurants, bazaars, people and performances. I absorbed and incubated new ideas. But he also knew I didn't write when I traveled. How was I to birth my first novel among the exuberant colors and exotic sounds of Mexico? I could not let my senses soak in and immerse themselves in Mexico's culture. I sighed, then sagged onto a chair.

"What is the problem?" he said. "I thought you would be thrilled."

I repeated my decision to write a novel in a month and explained the details.

"If we go, the Caribbean sun and sand will inspire you; you'll write better."

Huh? Wasn't he listening? He must have been thinking of some other writer.

"I cannot create in full sunlight. My muses visit only in my study through the narrow window that faces west. By the time the sun reaches it, I am finished for the day."

I shared my anxiety. "I don't want to go! The idea of this novel is churning inside me. It is ready to come out on the first day of next month."

"Delivery would be better in beautiful surroundings, trust me!"

I did not know what to say; I had to think.

"I have booked a room in a luxury resort that overlooks the sea. You don't have to write in your study all the time. You can write on the balcony the first thing in the morning; you can go for solitary walks on the beach whenever you want."

Easy for him to say! "And what will you do?" I asked.

"I will read when you write and walk quietly beside you when you walk the beach. I won't mind. Trust me, it'll be fun!" I gazed at his face. He was expecting me to say yes. I didn't have the heart to say no to such a loving offer.

With trepidation, I packed the carefully written outline of a yet-to-be-titled novel. On October 30, we left for Cancun.

The sound of waves hitting the beach woke us early. I sat on the porch facing the ocean and admired the November seascape, sunny and warm in Playa del Carmen. Then I sat to write and did not stop until my shadow had moved to my left. To my surprise, I had written more than one thousand, six hundred, sixty-six words.

At lunch, we feasted on freshly cut papaya and kiwi, omelet, pork tortillas, spinach and celery juice, fried plantains, and Mexican coffee. After window-shopping at the colorful Playa del Carmen craft market overflowing with tourists, we returned to the beach and walked on the white sand before dinner. For the next three days, I closely followed the outline that had taken me a month to write, rewrite, revise, and finalize.

By the fourth day, however, I felt that the outline was not working. Unwilling to admit so to myself, I reread what I had written so far. It was all wrong! The story had lost its intensity. The beautiful surroundings seemed to have sucked the life from it. The characters were lifeless. I was nervous. Had I written seven thousand useless words? I panicked and doubted my ability to complete the project in the time allotted. But I did not say a word to my husband.

That evening, with a discouraged heart and confused mind, I accompanied my husband for a walk on the beach. I walked barefoot in tepid waves over the warm sand. If the old outline was out, what was I going to write? I looked at the sky. Dark clouds were pushing the lighter gray ones away, and it started to drizzle.

"Let's run to the hotel!" my husband said and started to run. "It's going to rain!" "I know! You go ahead. I don't mind getting wet," I said, gazing at the thick dark clouds loosening up and pouring rain onto the lapping waves.

He stopped. "Are you okay?"

"I'm fine. You go; I'll see you back in the room."

"Are you sure?"

"Yeah, sure, I'll be okay."

He knows to leave me alone when I am in one of my moods. Soon it started to pour. Surrounded by darkness and feeling empty inside, I walked at a snail's pace. Then a visceral thought came to me: I am a seed enveloped in a nourishing shell of elements. Dark sky, dark atmosphere, dark earth. Together they were amalgamating psychic material; a new idea was being born. Thunder rolled. My imagination pushed away mundane thoughts. With my shifting thoughts at bay, my mind cleared and my heart filled with emotions. A calm spread over my body. My thoughts were crystal clear—as clear as the silence and solitude of my study.

It poured heavily for a few minutes, and then suddenly stopped. I was washed from head to toe. My mind was as clear as the sky where it met the horizon, gently kissing the deep blue of the sea. Out of the two blues emerged a name: "Arthur Zapata." I stood still as I felt a presence at the core of my being. I was awake yet in a state of sweet slumber. The image of Arthur pushed my thoughts about that lifeless outline aside.

The next day, while riding the bus to Chichen Itza, it seemed as if Arthur Zapata sat beside me. As the blue sky and green trees rushed by at sixty miles an hour, I could hear his story. He traced his ancestry to the sixteenth-century and the Spaniards. His Spanish father had married a Mayan woman and moved to the United States when Arthur was two. When he was in middle school, with a budding artistic mind, Arthur asked his father about the senseless destruction of the Mayan culture by the Spaniards. His father replied that that's how history goes: big fish eat little fish.

That was no answer. Finding the reasons for one civilization destroying another—in particular discovering what happened to the Mayans and why—became Arthur's life's mission. He received his master's degree in anthropology from Harvard and a PhD in South American archaeology from the University of Mexico; then he went to work for the Ministry of Archaeology and Anthropology.

Arthur worked for forty years, researching, teaching, and writing books, earning a name for himself as a great archaeologist and historian. His book on the symbolism of carvings at Palenque, on the west coast of Mexico, is considered a classic on Mayan archaeology and art. After he retired, his wife died, leaving him a lonely widower. A few months following his father's death, his mother died too. What brought passion into his life were the discoveries he dug out of the ancient sites. As a retiree, he had time on his hands, and he often pondered the meaning of his life.

Several years after retirement, an invitation arrived from the government of Mexico asking him to help a team of archaeologists digging at a site in the Yucatan Peninsula. The team had excavated an underground chamber with painted walls containing two skeletons, a hieroglyphic stone frieze, painted pottery, and jade and gold artifacts. The invitation felt like a call to Arthur.

Frantically, I wrote down all that seemed to appear to me from nowhere in a notebook that I carried. I wrote in our hotel room, on the bus, and sitting on a stone slab amid the ruins.

While viewing the breathtaking Cenote filled with deep water at the ancient site of Chichen Itza, another name echoed in my ears: "Regina, Regina Quintana."

Over the course of the following days, Regina Quintana's character blossomed. She had graduated with honors from Yale and gone to Mexico City to teach. Nearing forty and charming, she was a professor of Mayan art history at the University of Mexico. She had been born and raised in the town of Playa del Carmen. Mayan artworks, architecture, and traditions fascinated her, especially the ritualistic decapitation of athletes after a ball game. Solving the mystery of the relationship between royalty and athletes had become her lifelong challenge, even sacrificing having a family for a successful career.

Now at the peak of her profession, she felt emotionally unfulfilled. What she had achieved seemed of no consequence. Her biggest regret was that she had never married and had children. In the flurry of her professional climb, she had not realized how quickly time was passing.

She joined the team of archeologists who had invited Arthur because of her expertise in the Mayan rituals of death and decapitation. It seemed that the two skeletons they had unearthed had been decapitated.

For the next several days, I wrote feverishly.

At the exquisite seaside city of Tulum, my head filled with the circumstances surrounding Arthur and Regina's first encounter. What kind of people were they? Where would they meet and what would be the reason for their meeting? Our guide was of Mayan ancestry and proud of it. A few inches taller than five feet, he had dark skin and dove-grey eyes. He enthusiastically narrated the history of Tulum for the international tourists in Spanish, French, and English.

I had written about twenty thousand words of the new story line. The next day, I carried the old, dead outline to the shore. Standing knee deep in seawater and feeling fearless, I tore up the pages and scattered them on the receding waves. Not a bit floated back.

The next day, we returned home.

A day after our arrival, my husband flew to Carlsbad, California, on a business trip. I had several full days to write, but my muse was dormant. Was the end of our trip the end of Arthur and Regina's story? I meditated. Read. Drew pencil sketches. Cooked. Then amidst my normal activity, Arthur and

Regina shyly and slowly came back to life, visiting me in my own kitchen.

Unknown to each other, they were staying in the same hotel, the one my husband and I had stayed in, Paradise Resort. Both the hero and heroine of my novel had received calls to adventure. At first, they refused to pay heed to that call. Ultimately, each one felt a pull from something that impelled them towards this adventure. Arthur thought this last dig might help him find an answer to the question of why civilizations destroy one another. Regina believed that interacting with a group of archaeologists might help further boost her career, which seemed to have hit a dead end. Each character felt unfulfilled in some way and accepted the invitation as a search to fill that void. I wrote about their meeting and how they connected psychologically in the hotel's restaurant.

Four thousand words in two long sessions.

On the night of November 21, our daughter called to say that she was in labor and leaving for the hospital. Excited about the news but anxious about Arthur and Regina, I drove to my daughter's home in Virginia. While driving, thoughts of another character emerged: Diego Cervantes, a highly talented academician with an emotionally cold persona, the result of the death of his young wife whom he had adored. He looked very much like our guide at the city of Tulum. In Cervantes's younger years, he worked as a tour guide and freelance archaeologist and he spent much of his time puzzling over ancient hieroglyphics. Now he was a full-fledged Mayan linguist. As he was making wall rubbings of hieroglyphs at Palenque, he was summoned to Chichen Itza to join the team of American and Mexican archaeologists. He too refused at first, but when he saw that Arthur Zapata was on the team, he changed his mind and put his own work on hold. From the day he had graduated from college, Diego had admired Arthur, whose books he used in his research papers.

Diego's job was to decipher the hieroglyphic stone frieze that had been discovered along with other artifacts. When the work started, Arthur invited one of his best teaching assistants, Sara Singh, to help with his findings. Although an academic scholarship holder, Sara was rather naïve about anything not related to her work and studies.

Yes! This was the direction my novel needed to go. By this time, I had written about forty thousand words.

We were blessed with a beautiful granddaughter on November 22. While babysitting my four-year-old grandson, I continued to write my daily quota when he took his afternoon naps. I realized that although I had thought the only place I could write was a geographic space with a narrow window facing west. Instead, I learned that I could write from a place deep within me, a creative center where my sacred self resides.

On Thanksgiving Day, our daughter came home, lovingly holding the new baby. My husband joined us as we celebrated the joyous day with a sumptuous dinner. The following days, I continued to write as much as I could.

For months, Regina, Arthur, Diego, and Sara examined, studied, translated, traced, sketched, and photographed the excavated treasure. In the process of unearthing the Mayan relics, they discovered their own inner shadows and strengths. They realized that they were not who they thought they were. In varying degrees, they experienced their true natures. They felt inner changes and began to grow from them.

Arthur realized that there was no specific answer to the question about the meaning of his life. He had passionately asked the question: What is the meaning of human existence? When the answers he found began to hurt, he did not shove them away, but willingly received them. Despite the human dilemma, Arthur found happiness.

Regina's desire to experience womanhood was fulfilled. She stirred good feelings in Diego and broke the shell he had built around his heart after the death of his wife, who had died giving birth to their first child, a stillborn. In time he revealed an exuberant personality and took an interest in Regina's life.

Watching Arthur, Regina, and Diego at work and at play, Sara learned that there was life besides work, that dedication to work and passion for life were ultimately the same—individual yearning. The ideal is to find the balance.

At my daughter's home, I wrote more words in a day than I had ever written before. Location was irrelevant, as my subconscious flew through my fingertips. Relaxed and not the least bit self-conscious, I wrote my debut novel, one that no one else could have written. My muses did travel! In unfamiliar terrain, they inspired me. They were every bit as active as when I wrote in the comfort of my study.

On the last day of November, I had written more than sixty thousand words, enough for a novella. I titled it *The Meaning of Our Lives*. I pondered over the meaning of my own life while writing this piece. Some days it disturbed me, other days it made me fearful, but in the end, it freed me. The theme of the novel and its story line made me write things that I previously had been unable to express.

It is comforting to know that my muses travel—that even in foreign surroundings they inspire, and that they can be every bit as active as when I am at home. I also realized that my latest writing was the reflection of my own change, my own growth. I discovered that, deep within, I carry my creative energy in a portable shrine.

A BOOK CLUB GUIDE

The suggested questions are included to enhance your group's reading of Madhu Bazaz Wangu's *Chance Meetings: Stories About Cross-Cultural Karmic Collisions and Compassion*

Discussion Questions

1. In "Cycle of Life" the protagonist while growing up is a social rebel. Have you ever sensed the meaninglessness of life? How did you deal with that feeling?

2. What is the secret of Valakya's equipoise and wisdom? How does it help him face the fear of death?

3. Have you come across a relationship in your life as abusing as that of Saras and his boss? At some point, did the abused meet someone like the "Secret Healer?"

4. How can Mrs. Weiss be so graceful and yet so prejudiced?

5. What would you do if you find yourself facing a similar family situation as that of Gauri in "Gauri's Freedom?"

6. Whom does the protagonist of "The Blackened Mirror" see in the mirror?

7. Do you think the protagonist of this story was right in accusing "The Thug?"

8. Do you feel free to talk about death with someone close to you the way protagonist of "A Precious Gift" talks with her mother?

9. Did you ever have "A Chance Meeting?" Did it enhance or endanger your life?

10. Do you know someone who died young or unexpectedly as in "Yellow Jacket" and "A Precious Gift?" How did it affect you? Did it make you feel guilty or fearful of your own death?

11. What is the downfall of illiteracy in a culture or an individual? Were you deeply desirous of something early in your life as Lyn, the protagonist of "Darkness Behind Eyes," was but the circumstances kept you from achieving it?

12. In what ways does your experience of meeting someone by chance parallel with some stories in the collection?

13. Which characters from these stories do you most admire? Which do you find least admirable? And why?

14. Have some of the stories helped you deepen your views about art and spirituality? What part does art or religion play in your life?

15. Why does the author of *The Chance Meetings* tell several stories from first person point of view?

Coming Soon…

An Immigrant Wife

(A Novel)

CHAPTER ONE
AN IMMIGRANT WIFE

Late 1957, The Valley of Kashmir, India.

With the lower Himalayan ranges in the background, the valley of Kashmir was often compared to Switzerland. Locals as well as visitors who came throughout the year in throngs were enchanted by its changing seasons. In winter, the snow covered the peaks and the earth. But in early spring purple crocuses sprouted through the melting snow, giving way to almond and cherry blossoms. Then came the blooming season of tulips, daffodils, and gladioli. In summer, dahlia and chrysanthemums covered the ground until the chinar trees turned from green to gold to rust and once again the valley turned to stillness and silence of white. The rust and pewter leaves floated under the seven bridges that joined its banks like siblings holding hands.

Shanti Bamzai thanked the Great Goddess, *Devi* for creating the glorious valley on earth that was her home. On a sunny summer morning she was seated cross-legged on the balcony that jutted out of the study room overlooking River Jehlum. She wanted to sketch the familiar landscape as its view had changed with the new season. But her morning was spoilt, like a baby cockroach creeping on a plate of steaming white rice. Her father, Bubb had suggested she marry the boy he had found for her. Caught off guard, Shanti, usually articulate, could not think of a thing to say to Bubb. She knew he loved her as dearly as her older siblings, Gaurav and Ganga. But the proposal came out of the blue and pestered her.

I don't want to marry someone I have not even met and live like a caged bird! I want to go to an art college! The resolution helped Shanti replace the feeling of powerlessness with positive energy. She pushed the strand of hair behind her ear and tried to focus on sketching. If she married this stranger, as Bubb had commanded, everything would change. Bubb was an orthodox man, a traditionalist. If any one in the family talked against the time honored customs and conventions he lost his temper, or worse still, stopped talking to that person. Shanti was at odds with conventions. She was weary of meaningless rites and rituals, as was her brother, Gaurav. After an elaborate wedding ceremony, she would have to live with her groom in an unfamiliar household. Her freedom to make art would be curbed and replaced by drudgery. She would be bogged down with cooking and cleaning and sewing and shopping, the way Maji had been when she married Bubb.

The best hours of Maji's day were spent doing routine household chores. Maji still had not finished embroidering the dining spread she had enthusiastically started a year ago. She had selected silk threads to embroider flowers, birds and butterflies. She had imagined the design, had the fabric, and threads in rainbow colors, yet she could not make visible what was in her imagination. She did not have time. The drudgework and her family responsibilities always took precedence.

Ganga, Shanti's older sister, whom she called Didi, was so much like Maji. Not in looks but their interests were similar. Ganga liked to shop and clean and cook, but had no other ambition. She would love being married and would be a great wife and mother. But that was not what Shanti imagined her life to be. She wanted to become an artist.

The thought disturbing her floated away as she got absorbed in sketching the row of three-storied uneven mud houses on the opposite side of the river. The skyline of the rooftops was sharp against the early noon sky. The river splashing gently against the foundation of the houses was partly hidden but clearly visible to her. Over its blue water *shikara* boats carried passengers across the river. A few boats sailed towards the seventh bridge, in the direction of the boulevard business district—the heart of the capital city. Many others sailed in the opposite direction. The River Jehlum streamed through the heart of the valley of Kashmir spotted with fresh water springs. Rivulets gurgled under the swishing chinars and poplars as maina and koyal birds nested on their branches.

Shanti completed the riverscape and kept it aside. To keep her mind occupied, she sketched the silhouette of a woman seated firmly on a docked boat. It took less time to finish. She tilted her head to examine it. This one was better then the previous one. She rested her hand on the sketchpad and stared at the distant mountain peaks.

She did not know where her desire to become an artist came from. But the desire was deep and it drove her to draw every day. An inner prompting coaxed her to put ideas and images on paper. She wanted to make great art—not to become famous or wealthy or leave a legacy, but to pour out on paper that which floated in her imagination and in her heart. Where her family members saw nothing, she saw beauty. Where they saw ugliness she saw shapes and colors. She saw what no one else saw. Her vision was different from other people's vision. In the river below she noticed shimmering reflections, water receding, surface glittering from the sun's rays. The others did not; they were busy walking, talking, reading, listening to radio. How could they not see all this beauty around them?

The gnawing in her belly, she had managed to ignore so far, returned. *I'll marry when I'm ready, and after I graduate from Shantiniketan. I don't want to sacrifice my dream into the fire of marriage. I love Bubb and it pains me to disappoint him. But giving up painting would be like stopping to breathe. No wedlock for me.*

Earlier that morning, Bubb's announcement about the most suitable match for her had buckled her knees. Did Bubb mean it? Would he insist? Would he force the match upon her? She knew if she refused, he would stop talking to her for days. It was better to get Gaurav Bhaiya's advice. She called him Bhaiya out of respect because he was older, nine years older, forward looking and open minded. He taught Math and Physics at the University of Kashmir. Gaurav's values and beliefs clashed with those of Bubb, who followed traditions whether reasonable, logical or not. No exceptions. No questions asked.

"What about Ganga Didi?" Shanti had asked Bubb, "I thought you and Maji were on the hunt for a boy for her?"

Bubb thumped his head. "Why do you talk like that? We are indeed looking for a boy for your sister. With the grace of the Great Goddess, we'll receive another offer. But this offer seems good for you, why refuse?"

Shanti looked straight into her father's eyes. "But Didi is seven years older than me! I am not ready to marry!"

"We can't wait for seven years! Such offers don't come every day." Bubb sounded agitated. "This boy is young for Ganga, but perfect for you. He has a government job and will get a good pension. He is a Sarasvat Brahmin, same caste as ours, and good looking. You'll be set for life!"

But it's not you who is getting married, Bubb. It's me, and I refuse! Shanti wanted to scream but restrained herself. She wished her father could read her thoughts because she did not have the courage to tell him the future she had imagined for herself.

"I want to go to college like Bhaiya and Didi did." Shanti made herself say aloud.

"What good did the four years of college do for your sister? She is getting married and will lead a life like your mother. Maji never went to college!"

"Maji got married when she was twelve—she was not given the choice, she didn't know any better."

"And you do? Calm down, *Kuri*, daughter! Be warned, as soon as we find a boy for Ganga, you should be prepared." He said and then added fondly, "Won't it be nice if we have a double wedding?"

Shanti knew that Bubb worried for his children, especially his daughters. What if they don't find a suitable match? What if they remain unmarried and lose their way? What if they end up marrying out of caste? Such questions circled his mind and stole his sleep.

Shanti stared at the father she loved but no longer recognized. This was the reason she disliked his blind faith. Even before a girl passed puberty the parents were ready to send her away if they found a suitable boy. The daughter's opinion did not count. She was not given an opportunity to flourish. *An arranged marriage? For Bubb's convenience? So that his two responsibilities are over with one shot? Had he consulted Maji?* Bubb was like a bolted door, once his mind was shut, no force could open it. Except perhaps, Gaurav Bhaiya.

Bhaiya encouraged Ganga and Shanti to read Hindi and English books: Premchand's *Godan*, Tagore's *Gitanjali,* Irving Stone's *Lust for Life* and *Agony and Ecstasy*. Maji read the scriptures of the great goddess, *Bhagavad Gita* and *Devi Gita.* Bubb read the epics *Mahabharata* and *Ramayana.* Neither the ancient texts nor the modern books had anything to say about arranged marriages. They reflected on the nature of gods and goddesses, about fulfilling responsibility, leading a meaningful life, about death, afterlife and such matters. But nothing about arranged marriage. In fact readings from goddess texts empowered Shanti.

The goddess Radha—Krishna's beloved was passionate and daring. She traversed serpent-infested paths at night in thunderstorm and rain to meet her lover. Shanti meticulously drew the entwined bodies of Radha and Krishna attired in yellow and red embellished with gold jewelry. Drawing such images stirred pleasurable feelings in her.

Maji had set down miniature statues of gods with their consorts: Radha and Krishna, Sita and Ram, Shiva and Parvati, Vishnu and Lakshmi, and Durga in her shrine. The shrine, made of walnut wood, sat in one corner of the dining room facing the kitchen. Maji hummed songs about Radha's longing for Krishna. Would she not get angry if Shanti left home in the middle of the night to meet a boy? Shanti asked her mother. Her jaw fell open. With her hand on her mouth she looked at her precocious teenage daughter and said, "Child, the union of the divine couple is a metaphor for the union between a devotee and a deity. Radha is not an ordinary woman. She exemplifies the impediments a devotee confronts on the path to God. Radha's story is not meant to encourage you to run away from home in terrible weather to meet your imaginary boyfriend!"

Remembering Maji's rebuke made Shanti smile. Her attention was brought back to her drawing when she heard Bhaiya enter the house. She gathered her drawing materials and walked down the balcony and entered the study room that Bubb shared with Bhaiya.

Bubb was seated cross-legged in his woolen *pheran*, his knee-length cloak. He felt most comfortable wearing it over pajama pants that Maji had stitched. He was sitting against a cylindrical cushion on the carpeted floor in front of his low desk. The lidded desk stored a holder with nib, an inkpot, pencils, a stack of blank paper, textbooks reminiscent of his years as a middle school teacher. In the wall facing him was an alcove enshrined with the miniature statues of gods and goddesses. The floor was covered with a handmade carpet woven by the world famous Kashmiri craftsmen. In the left corner stood a four-foot walnut lamp that lit Bubb's desk. A lit hookah sat to his right.

Hearing her brother enter the room emboldened Shanti. In his presence she could talk fearlessly. He encouraged her to speak her mind. Her voice firm but her eyes lowered she said, "I don't want to marry, Bubb!"

Gaurav came into the room, nodded at his father and sister, pulled out the chair from his study table and sat. All the furniture on his side of the study had legs. His generation of Kashmiris did not sit on the floor but had western style table and chairs. Gaurav's table held two stacks of books, a pile of files, a typewriter, and a papier-mâché penholder with several red and blue pens and pencils. Prominently displayed on a side table was a bust of the Buddha. He swiveled his chair to face Bubb and Shanti, and listened.

Bubb took a long puff from the hookah beside him. The smell of sweet tobacco filled the room. "What do you want to do with your life? Remain unmarried?"

"I want to go to Shantiniketan." Shanti lifted her chin and looked at her brother. He knew her sole desire was to go to the art school at Shantiniketan in Bengal. Just saying the word "Shantiniketan" transported her to a place of mystery and beauty, a world of vast open spaces, palm trees and brilliant constellations. Rabindranath Tagore, India's first Nobel Laureate poet had founded the school. Every year some of the world's most creative minds gathered there. Shanti imagined herself communing with nature, enjoying the companionship of talented art students and learning from the best art teachers.

Bubb sneered, replacing his hookah pipe. "Shantiniketan? In Bengal?" He sat up, looking straight at his son.

"Have they opened another one elsewhere?" Gaurav winked at his baby sister.

"*Hee Divi*!" Bubb said invoking the Great Goddess. "You put all these ideas into her head. Why would a smart girl like her want to go to a college so far away? Why can't she put her energy into some good use, get married, make a home—happy husband, happy boys, stable life?" He frowned.

"That's what Maji did and look…" Shanti said as she looked at her brother who had raised an eyebrow. She stopped talking.

"Instead of encouraging her to learn cooking and household chores from her mother you encourage her to make lines and shapes. Rejecting a fine match! When did she get so bold and rude?"

"She has been always bold, Bubb, not—I would not say she is rude." A year ago Gaurav had given Shanti an artist's kit. Since then the family, except Bubb, had viewed with pleasure semblances of their surroundings on her drawing pad.

"Rejecting a suitable boy for some faraway place to learn to draw!" Bubb must have felt a chill because he slipped a lit *kangri*, an earthenware bowl in a frame of wickerwork, under his loose *pheran* and embraced it against his body. The population of the valley was ninety-five percent Muslim and only five percent Hindu. The marriage alliances were strictly religious but what if Shanti wanted to marry one of them? Bubb considered Muslims a low caste, or no-caste people—destitute, dirty, labor class. How could a Sarasvat Brahmin family like his have anything to do with them. The sooner Shanti was married, the less chance there was of a thing like that happening.

"What beloved is to a lover's bosom, *kangri* is to a Kashmiri." Gaurav recited a local saying to lighten the mood.

"Stop changing the subject, son!"

Gaurav shrugged, "Education cultivates minds, Bubb. Besides, what are you afraid of? She has a good head on her shoulders."

"Why does she have to go so far away to learn how to draw? Things would be different if she was...."

Gaurav held his chin between his thumb and index finger. "Because she wants to learn from the best teachers and hone her god... no her goddess-given talent."

"Who knows whom she'll meet there," Bubb said, his forehead lined from disgust. "Will you be happy if she ends up marrying a Muslim boy?" He got up, shaking the daily paper in his hand.

"What are you talking about?" Gaurav said.

Bubb tapped at a news item in the paper. A Hindu girl had run away with a Muslim boy she met in college. The whole city was in an uproar.

"You know how they are!" Bubb grumbled and sat down. There were as many affluent Muslims who lived in the Valley of Kashmir, as there were poor Muslims, the majority of them middle class. But Bubb did not interact with any of them except the people who came to clean the latrine or carry a bundle of dirty clothes to wash. Therefore he considered the whole Muslim population as lowly people.

"We live in *Kala Yuga*, the age of the Kali, that's what we live in! Our daughters marrying *their* sons, *Hee Divi*!"

"Whose? Muslims?"

"Who else?" Bubb said, raising his voice.

Gaurav clicked his tongue. "I'm sure somewhere out there, an orthodox Muslim is badmouthing Hindus."

"What can they say about Hindus?" Bubb said.

"I don't want to get into *that* argument," Gaurav said. "Believe it or not, fine Muslim boys do exist. So what, if Shanti marries one of them." He looked sideways at her.

"Get your head examined!" Bubb snapped raising his right hand in a fist as his forehead wrinkled. "*Hee Divi*! Why have you kept me alive in this dark Age?"

"I would have married Radhika even if she were Muslim." Gaurav sighed.

"If you had married a Muslim girl, do you think I would have let you enter this house?" Bubb paused, clearly waiting for a retort from one of the two. When they did not respond he broke the silence by turning to Shanti. "Until yesterday you couldn't even look into my eyes. Today you are talking back to me. Where did you learn all this?" Taking a long puff from his hookah, he asked his son, "Do you want me to return the marriage proposal? Is that what you want?" Then again he said to Shanti, "Is this how a good daughter treats her father…. talks back to him?" He paused for a few moments. Then he said, "Have you talked to your mother?"

"Maji wants me to go to college as much as *she* wanted to go!" Shanti said in one breath.

"*Hey Divi, Hey Divi!* I raised you, and this is how you treat me? " Bubb shouted, a nerve on his neck palpitating.

His orthodox worldview unsettled Shanti; she could not keep her mouth shut.

"Raised me? Like a tree growing in the forest!"

"What? What did you say?" Bubb said.

Gaurav motioned Shanti to leave the room. "Nothing, Bubb, nothing important!"

Bubb took another long puff from his hookah, making the coal in the terracotta *chillum* burn red and the water gurgle and grunt. Maji always kept a window cracked open to let the stale smoke escape. Through the crack Shanti heard the river flow.

What's the use? I'll rather talk to Maji and let her talk to him, thinking thus she left the study.

A garden patch separated the main house from the study room with the balcony. In one half of the garden Maji planted marigolds and roses and in the other half green mint and red chilies. She harvested the former for the adoration of her deities and the latter for the pleasure of her family. In the first floor of the house, the kitchen and the dining room facing the kitchen were Maji's domain.

Walking up a few steps to the main house, Shanti inhaled the aroma coming through the dining room windows. The two bay windows with lattice shutters overlooked the garden patch and the river, as did the windows of the three bedrooms on the second floor. But the family's favorite view was from the bay windows with beautifully carved wooden lattice shutters.

At dinnertime, the Bamzai family, except for Gaurav's wife Radhika, visiting her parents, sat around the dinner spread on the straw floor mat. Furniture was unnecessary. How could one eat seated on a chair? Ganga Didi, who looked glamorous even in her home clothes, was seated in front of Shanti. The family sat comfortably cross-legged around the white cotton sheet that had yellowed over the years. Maji had embroidered its charming multicolored border with a pattern of birds and flowers the first year of her marriage.

"Shanti, did you hear?" Maji said from the kitchen. "Priyanka is getting married to a boy from *Amreekah.*" Kitchen shelves held earthenware and stainless steel cooking vessels, jars of grain and stone and wood mortars and pestles for grinding and husking.

Bubb gave a hard stare at Shanti. "A nice Hindu boy from her community. The way it should be!"

"He lives in America, but the marriage was arranged in the old fashioned way," Gaurav said. He was not particularly happy about Priyanka's marrying so young. He took pride in encouraging his sisters to get educated, be self-dependent and to make right choices.

Shanti raised her head, glanced at Maji and Ganga and then turned to Bubb.

"Priyanka wants to marry, Bubb, I don't. Why are you forcing your wish on me?"

Shanti's recent behavior must have bothered Bubb. He wanted his daughters to behave like nice Kashmiri girls. He didn't like his son's liberating influence on them and was hurt by what Shanti had just said. The more she talked about going to college, the stricter he became. But Shanti thought the so-called "nice" girls behaved like puppets. Too afraid to express their true feelings, they let their budding dreams or desires be smothered by tradition, snatched away by conformity.

Since Shanti had turned sixteen, some girls in her class had been persuaded to quit school and marry. Most accepted a girl's "fate," felt a few panged for sacrificing their carefree youth, but could not or did not do anything to keep their freedom. Shanti admired Didi's attitude. At the ripe old age of twenty-three she had announced that she was going to live a life she desired. *So would I*, Shanti thought as she said to Ganga. "Do you know Bubb is searching for a "suitable boy" for you?"

Ganga was placing bronze plates and glasses on the sheet. She did not reply to Shanti's question. Instead she turned to her father and said, "Why don't you let Shanti go to Shantiniketan, Bubb? I went to college."

Shanti beamed.

"This is nothing to smile about." Bubb glared at Shanti. Then turning to Ganga he said, "But *kuri*, daughter, you did not leave the valley. I still think Shanti's going away is a big mistake. And I don't want to talk about it anymore." He took a few big gulps of water and pointed to his glass for more. "By the way, Ganga, I have not talked to your mother yet…but I have someone in mind for you…." Maji filled Bubb's glass with water.

Shanti thought Bubb couldn't be talking about the same boy he had suggesting for her. *Wouldn't he be too young for her? Did he have another match for Ganga Didi?*

"Bubb! No more marriage proposals, please!" Gaurav said.

"You've someone in mind for me, Bubb?" Ganga looked wide-eyed at Bubb and turned to Maji.

"Listen, you all! Thanks to Lord *Ganesh* and Ganga's good luck, I've good news!" Maji said as she served steaming rice.

"Good luck? What are you saying?" Bubb said.

"What I'm saying is, college was no 'big mistake' for Ganga. There, she met the Razdan boy."

"Who?" Bubb sounded confused.

With a smile on her face Maji looked at each one of them and said, "Bansi Pandit brought a marriage proposal for Ganga from Razdan family."

Bubb thumped his head. "Why wasn't I told before you talked to the matchmaker? Why am I the last one to know?"

"You had gone for your evening prayers to the temple when the matchmaker paid us a visit." The room fell silent. Everyone looked at Ganga, whose face flushed and gaze lowered.

Bansi Pandit, the matchmaker, had come to the Bamzais' home with a marriage proposal on the Razdan family's behalf. He charged his clients based on their income: the richer the client the more commission they gave him. Usually when he negotiated marriage between two families it took some time and effort. But this proposal was an easy deal.

Shanti was as much surprised as Bubb. When they heard the news, all burst into conversation. Shanti came over and hugged her sister from behind. Gaurav, seated next to Ganga, put his arm around her shoulders and squeezed her gently.

Maji served fresh kale, fragrant with mustard oil, and lamb roganjosh of the color of the roasted pomegranate. White rice and frothy buttermilk in glasses completed the meal.

"What has a marriage proposal to do with going to college?" Bubb asked before putting the next morsel of rice in his mouth.

"If Ganga Bamzai had not met Neel Razdan at college, how would a retired schoolteacher's daughter receive a marriage proposal from a prosperous family like Razdans?" Maji said.

Bubb nodded thoughtfully. Shanti knew that the idea of a connection with the Razdan family through marriage and the elevated social status of their family that it would bring had pleased him greatly.

At breakfast the next morning, Ganga asked Bubb, "So, what have you decided?"

"About what?"

"About letting Shanti go to the college of her choice, the way I did."

"But *kuri*, you came home every evening." Bubb pointed toward Shanti. "She wants to leave the valley – mother Kashir-- to go to some godforsaken place! Where does she hear about foreign places like these?"

Ganga grunted. "Shantiniketan is in India, Bubb."

Maji served sweet black tea from a steaming samovar with *chot*, unleavened bread lathered with hot butter. "When something gets stuck in your head you refuse to think beyond it," she whispered to her husband.

As a young girl Maji did not know about art schools. She would have attended one if she had a choice. Betrothed at nine and married at twelve, she saw herself in her daughters. She wanted them to follow their dreams, as had their son. Gardening and embroidering were her way to "paint" her dreams.

"What do you know?" Bubb said to his wife, raising his voice. "Your world revolves around your kitchen." When she glared at him he turned to Shanti. "Why do I waste time talking to you all?"

Shanti whispered to Maji, "Please don't say anything. You'll make him angrier."

Then she turned to her father, "Aren't you glad, Bubb, Didi found her own match?"

He waved his hand and ignored her. She was expecting it, yet saddened by it. As the family conversed about Neel Razdan's family, it suddenly struck to Shanti that she had talked to Maji and Bubb like a grown up. She sat up straight feeling proud. From now on she need not raise her voice or argue. If she disagreed she would discuss like an adult with a sense of humor if she could. In any case she can give reasons, let the other person know why she saw things differently.

Bubb had not said much to her since she declared her decision not to marry but go to college. Was there a way to convince him that it was the best way for her?

Early Praise for
An Immigrant Wife

Beautiful and lush, *An Immigrant Wife* takes the reader on one woman's touching, turmeric-drenched journey from naive but determined art student in India to longing-filled American wife and mother. The author Madhu B. Wangu has written a maharaja's banquet for the senses.

Gwyn Cready
(RITA Award Winning Author)

In her debut novel, *An Immigrant Wife,* Madhu B. Wangu brings to life a mysterious time and place. The protagonist, Shanti, begins her life as an idealistic but naive girl from the valley of Kashmir. As the story unfolds in America, she learns to heed her desires and shape her life, no longer rolling along like a stone turned in the tide. Wangu creates rich, dynamic images of India, comparable to her watercolors, evoking every sense. The indigenous sights, sounds, and smells are so vivid that I swear I could find my way to Shanti's home. Wangu's style is gentle and quiet like the protagonist, and deeply powerful. This tale of love and nurturing, loss and growth, and transformation will stay with readers long after they finish the novel.

Kathleen Shoop
(IPPY Award Winner)

An Immigrant Wife reminds me of *Emily Alone* by Stewart O'Nan. The story spans a much greater time period, but both novels deal with personal growth and life lessons, big and small. The author, Madhu B. Wangu, has written an enjoyable story and created unforgettable characters, especially the beautiful descriptions of art and the wonderful food descriptions. The author also skillfully portrays the artistic growth of the protagonist, Shanti, through her painting and cooking. This is a lovely, quiet story written lyrically.

Meredith Cohen
(Author, *Aftertaste*)

Shanti, the protagonist of *An Immigrant Wife*, is a sensitive artist forced to give up her passion for painting when she gets trapped in the cultural expectations of a wife and a mother. Reminiscent of Bharati Mukherjee's *Wife* (1975) and Monica Ali's *Brick Lane* (2003), the author, Madhu B. Wangu creates believable characters and places, Valley of Kashmir and New Delhi. Her local details of Pittsburgh are colorfully written.

Kirkus Review

www.ingramcontent.com/pod-product-compliance
Lightning Source LLC
Chambersburg PA
CBHW050146120726
47903CB00002B/516

* 9 7 8 1 6 4 6 4 9 3 4 8 7 *